Life in the
Valley

Additional copies of this book are available by calling toll-free 1-800-765-6955 or by visiting
www.AdventistBookCenter.com.

Library of Congress Cataloging-in-Publication Data
Names: Harvey, Susan Phelps, author.
Title: Life in the valley : one woman's journey to victory / Susan Phelps Harvey.
Description: Nampa : Pacific Press Publishing Association, 2017.
Identifiers: LCCN 2017006572 | ISBN 9780816362721 (pbk.)
Subjects: LCSH: Hamilton, Laura, 1957- | Seventh-Day Adventist converts—United States—
    Biography.
Classification: LCC BX6189.H36 H37 2017 | DDC 286.7092 [B] —dc23 LC record available
    at https://lccn.loc.gov/2017006572

ISBN 978-0-8163-6272-1

March 2017

Dear Lisa,
I hope my story and this book is
a great blessing to you and your
family. Love
Laura

Life in the
Valley
One Woman's Journey to Victory

SUSAN PHELPS HARVEY

Pacific Press®
Publishing Association
Nampa, Idaho | Oshawa, Ontario, Canada
www.pacificpress.com

A THANK-YOU FROM LAURA

One of the meanings of my first name is "she who sings of victory." I want to dedicate my story as a thank offering to my Lord Jesus Christ, who gave me that victory, rescued me from a life of pain and sorrow, and gave me an abundant life, full of peace and happiness. I thank Him for the great power He gave me to overcome the many bad habits and attitudes that nearly destroyed my life.

My deepest gratitude goes to my beloved husband, Greg, for his love, support, and encouragement throughout our marriage. I will always be grateful to Grandpa Duane Hamilton for judging me worthy to marry his grandson and to Ken and Verna Hamilton for adopting me as their daughter and loving me as their own.

I thank Dick Pollard, the evangelist who preached the Seventh-day Adventist message so that I could find the Lord and obtain the great freedom He gives. This truth has changed my life forever, and I am so grateful for the happiness I've found.

I thank Susan Harvey for writing my story and for her excellent skills, friendship, support, and encouragement in this effort. I thank my friend Pat Vivian for reviewing my story from a secular, humanist perspective and for providing suggestions to communicate more effectively with all members of society.

Laura Hamilton

TABLE OF CONTENTS

....

CHAPTER 1

············

"Too Bad It's Another Girl"

Laura Jane Sicking was born on September 11, 1957. Her mother, Mary, reached out eagerly as the child was placed in her arms, even though her face showed the exertion and pain of the last few hours.

Holding her infant close, she murmured a devout prayer, and her fingers automatically reached for the rosary that was always present on her bedside table. Mary Sicking was a complex person, and the force that controlled her life was her absolute devotion to the Catholic Church. She wanted God's blessing for this newest baby and vowed that the child would grow up to serve the church as a nun. Although Laura was the eighth child she had given birth to in the last eight years, Mary rejoiced in another new life.

Mary's purpose in life was to raise as large a family as possible in the Catholic faith. She believed that this was her path to salvation. Emmett, Laura's father, was less pleased about this child. He was a Texas dryland farmer, and he needed boys to help with the work around the place—not another female. He was a man of average height and weight, but somehow his presence filled the room as he strode through the door. He seemed to dwarf his wife and new baby as he looked at the two of them.

"Too bad it's another girl" were his first words. Then he looked down at his daughter's little face. He would love her, but the inner conflicts that drove him would make it difficult for her to know it.

Yet, Laura's first six years were happy ones. Her earliest memories were mostly of the outdoors—the fields, woods, and streams that shaped the large ranch where her family lived. By the time she was six, the family had grown to include three younger boys—Mark, Bryan, and Bill—for a total of eleven children, all born one year apart.

Bill, the newest baby, had been a month overdue. Mary's abdominal muscles were so weak and exhausted that normal labor and birth contractions were impossible, and her doctor had finally induced labor.

"Mrs. Sicking, having eleven children in as many years has taken a heavy toll on your health. If you get pregnant again, you could die," Dr. Kralick, the family doctor, told her when he saw her in the hospital after Bill was born. "You must let me tie your tubes."

"I can't do that!" Mary was shocked that her doctor suggested such a thing. He was Catholic, and he knew she was too. They both knew that birth control was a sin.

Dr. Kralick tried again. "If you don't allow me to do a tubal ligation, your next pregnancy will kill you and leave eleven children motherless! Is that what you want?"

Mary said nothing, refusing to meet his eyes. Mary left the hospital and visited her priest. She told him of her conversation with Dr. Kralick and requested the priest's permission to have her tubes tied.

"Mrs. Sicking, you know you can't get your tubes tied. If you get pregnant again and you die in childbirth, then that is God's will for you," the priest replied.

Mary Sicking left the priest's office in confusion. *I can't get pregnant again*, she thought. *I know I will die. Emmett can't raise eleven children.* It was an awful dilemma for a devout Catholic woman, but in the end, she had the tubal ligation.

Something in Mary changed after that. Always exceptionally pious, she became even more so, driven by the guilt about having her tubes tied. From then on, she went to Mass every day except Saturday and gave every spare penny to the church to make amends.

The family's ranch was a successful, thriving operation, at least in the drought-free years.

Emmett Sicking was a good farm manager and a hard taskmaster. He was proud of the 650-acre farm he owned, as well as the additional 1,200 acres of family land he managed. In time, he would rent the neighbor's 1,000-acre ranch.

Emmett and Mary were married in 1948, when Emmett was twenty-two and Mary was nineteen. When Emmett's dad died in 1950, Emmett received an inheritance of about ten thousand dollars, which he used to buy the farm. It had a small house on the property. So by most standards, they started out their marriage well-off. By the time Laura came along, the Sicking farm was prospering, and Emmett built a larger house to accommodate his growing family. It had four bedrooms and two bathrooms. One of the bathrooms was just for him, the father, and the other was shared by all of the children and their mother.

The first ten or so years of Emmett and Mary's marriage were good ones. As dryland farmers, the success of their farm was always dependent on the rains, but they had no debts, so life was generally good.

There was always a great deal of work to be done on the farm, and a big family was necessary to do it. The children worked hard milking the 150 cows; feeding and tending the 400 pigs, the 5,000 chickens, the 200 beef cattle, and the 2,850 acres of crops; along with helping to slaughter the animals; and working in the garden or in the machine shop—doing all of the hard, dirty tasks the big spread required. There were also other animals on the ranch, including three horses, a goat, a goose, a sheep, and a few rabbits. The children had fun playing with the animals while performing their chores. Laura named many of them, and they were her pets.

The older girls, Joan, Joyce, Debra, and Lois, milked the cows and toiled alongside their father in the fields. This process of milking the cows, even with machines, took three and a half hours each morning and evening—seven hours a day, seven days a week, rain or shine, school or no school. Virginia and Julie, who suffered from allergies to animals and hay, did the inside chores. One day Cliff, an older brother, accidently ate some of the lye the family used for making soap. Fortunately, Grandmother Sicking walked in at just the right time and saved his life. It was several years before Cliff was able to work on the farm again.

When Laura finished her chores, she escaped to the outdoors with her three younger brothers whenever possible. She loved the land, and she loved her father and looked up to him. There were good times when he would come in from the fields after a long day, still wearing his overalls, and invite her to sit on his knee. She would crawl up into his lap, and he would tickle her and tell her stories.

"How old are you, Laura?" he would ask.

"Hix!" she would reply with pride. He would roar with laughter at her childish mispronunciation, then urged her to repeat it over and over again.

Everyone on the farm had to work from a very young age. Their father made sure of that. Only someone raised on a ranch or a farm can imagine the kind of farmwork the children did and how young they started. All of the Sicking children learned to drive trucks, combines, and other farm equipment at what most people would consider an extremely young age.

Laura was only six and a half years of age when her dad taught her to drive the family's old farm truck. It took two pillows to prop her up—one to sit on and one behind her. Even though she was tall for her age, she could barely see over the steering wheel and reach the pedals.

As soon as she could manage the truck, she was promoted to the task of driving out to the northern forty acres every morning to wake up the cows, with her younger brother Bill as her helper. This chore involved the two children running through the herd, shouting, "Wake up, wake up," urging the 150 sleepy cows to go to the milking barn. Laura was excited, both to drive the truck and be given this grown-up responsibility. Every morning they would get up at four o'clock and drive to the most remote part of the family's ranch.

Bill was only three and a half when he became Laura's cow-waking assistant. They remained paired as working partners on the farm throughout their childhood. Bill was also tall for his age, dark eyed and dark haired, like their mother. And he was Laura's best pal. He loved the outdoors even more than she did. He liked to fish for crawdads in the creek and run free in the fields and woodlands, which were filled with opossums, raccoons, bobcats, and other wild animals. Laura and her three younger brothers had a lot of fun fishing and building a log cabin.

But there were coyotes in the northern forty acres, and they made their dens in the open fields. Bill was too young to be afraid of coyotes. Laura knew they were dangerous, and she knew she needed to keep one eye on Bill while they did their work.

One morning Laura suddenly realized she hadn't seen Bill for several minutes. Where was he? She stopped shouting at the cows and strained her eyes in every direction, trying to spot her little brother in the dark fields. Suddenly, she saw him. Bill was standing calmly in the pasture, surrounded by a pack of coyotes who were stealthily moving closer to him. Bill was oblivious to what was happening.

Laura's mother had warned her about coyotes. She knew they hunted in packs, moving in a circle, and when they got close enough, they would attack together. The animals were not much bigger than Bill; but together in a pack, they could easily kill a creature of his size or something even larger. Laura's heart beat fast. She could feel the panic rising and thought, *I have to do something to save Bill!*

Suddenly, she remembered that her mother had told her that coyotes were afraid of light. She ran back to the truck and turned on the headlights. But the coyotes ignored the light. Now what should she do? She couldn't just run toward Bill. The coyotes might attack them both. She wasn't much bigger than he was.

Without another thought, she started up the truck and drove it right into the coyote pack. "Bill," she yelled. "Get in the truck! Quick!" Bill jumped in, and they drove away as the coyotes scattered in all directions. Laura never told a soul about their close call with the coyotes. She was sure she would lose her driving privileges if anybody knew, and she didn't want that to happen!

Laura's family was German Catholic. They lived just outside the small farming community of Muenster, Texas. Muenster is about twelve miles south of the Texas-Oklahoma border and only about eighty miles from Dallas. The town is one of several small communities founded by German Catholics in the late 1800s. These immigrants were awarded large land grants by the Texas government to establish colonies.

These small groups of families had lived close together in Germany, and they tended to keep to themselves in Texas, maintaining their ethnicity and religion, building their own churches and schools, and speaking mostly German until World War II. They formed distinct, proud, and vibrant pockets of Old World culture, Catholic piety, and hardworking German values in the New World. Laura's parents and grandparents were a part of this culture.

She had no idea that her town was different from any other. As a child, she thought the kids in nearby towns talked funny, but she had no idea why.

Young Laura was raised to be a devout Catholic. She admired her mother's piety and goodness and wanted to emulate and please her in everything. From infancy, the children were instilled with a love for God and the Catholic Church by their mother. She often told Laura that she was to become a nun. Laura was too young to know what that meant, but she basked in the warmth of her mother's words. Laura loved the church with all of her heart. In her young mind, it was a symbol of goodness. She vowed to always be good so that she could someday serve the church and go to heaven.

All week Laura looked forward to Sunday Mass in Muenster's large and imposing Sacred Heart Catholic Church, which seats more than a thousand people. (Although the town is small, almost all of its citizens are Catholic.) The thundering pipe organ; the spicy-sweet smell of incense; the melodic singing; the Latin chants; the magnificent stone building with its golden chalices, marble floors, paintings, statues, and flickering candles all appealed to Laura's senses and her heart.

Laura learned to love God dearly, and somehow, although she wasn't taught to do so, she began to talk to Him as a friend. Throughout the day, as she and Bill roamed through the fields and woods or did their daily chores, God was their Companion. Laura found peace, joy, and happiness in God's presence. She had a very happy life with God by her side. She naturally turned to God for help when she needed it.

Laura prayed a lot. She prayed for clothes—always a scarce commodity. She prayed for toys at Christmas. And always, she felt that God was listening and that He answered her prayers.

She was a contented, sunny child, and this sense of God's nearness gave her a positive view of life at a very young age. As she grew older, when anguish and adversity threatened to overwhelm her, she would question God's existence. But having known Him on an intimate level as a child, she could never deny Him. Later in life, this early experience with God would drive her to find Him again.

So life for six-year-old Laura consisted mostly of hard work, outdoor fun with her little brothers, and a sense of being close to God and chosen for a special work in the Catholic Church. Because she spent most of her time outdoors with her brothers, she wasn't aware that there were any problems in the family. For her, life was good and quite happy, but soon everything would change.

CHAPTER 2

....

What Just Happened to Me?

During Laura's sixth year, there was little rain. The farm wasn't producing, and her dad was consumed with financial worries. He and their mother were broke, so broke that they were forced to buy groceries on credit at Black's Grocery Store in Myra, Texas.

Things got so bad that they were unable to pay their bills, and, for the second time in their marriage, Mary had to go to work at a factory in town, just so they would have food on the table. Having his wife work outside the home was something that felt very much like a personal failure to Emmett. With eleven children, mounting debts, and failing crops, he was under extreme stress.

Laura was oblivious to the family's problems until something very strange happened. Her father simply disappeared. Several years later she found out that he had a mental breakdown and was committed to the Wichita Falls State Hospital. The only thing she knew at the time, however, was that one day her dad was feeling ill and acting strangely. When he started having hallucinations, her mother called a neighbor and asked the neighbor to come to their house. Then her father was taken away.

It wasn't until Laura was an adult that she learned that this was the second time her father had had a psychotic episode, which was diagnosed as schizophrenia. His first stay in a mental hospital, she learned, occurred during an earlier downturn in the family fortunes, when she was two and a half, and it lasted only a few weeks.

At that time, he was given drugs to control his hallucinations and help him to manage his other symptoms. These drugs made him tired, irritable, and moody and had other adverse side effects that would compromise his health and cause him to develop an uncontrollable craving for sugar that led to excessive weight gain and other problems. It was a vicious cycle that continued to plague him throughout his life.

Emmett's eating habits became strange. He lived on an almost constant diet of soda and snack cakes. The family had two large chest freezers. One housed the normal household items, and the other was reserved exclusively for Emmett's Twinkies, Hostess Snack Cakes, and Ho Hos. He bought them by the bagful at the day-old bakery store for half price. The children weren't allowed to eat these things. Emmett Sicking's weight reflected his unhealthy diet. Before he was thirty-five, he ballooned to 350 pounds.

This second episode of mental illness was more serious, and Emmett was gone from home for several months. Laura's mother took over the farm management; and the children, trained to work hard and be responsible, ran the ranch without him. As previously mentioned, the lack of rain, failing crops, and continuing heavy expenses had hit the family's finances hard, forcing Mary to get a job at a sewing factory in town. The family needed her salary to make ends meet. So their mother was no longer home during the day.

One morning Laura, now six and a half years old, sat at the kitchen table, gazing out the window. Then she looked around the room with its bright yellow walls. It was the most cheerful room in the house, usually full of hustle and bustle, but this morning, it was empty, except for Laura.

After rising at 4:00 A.M. to wake the cows, Laura helped with feeding the calves and returned to the house to clean up. Her older siblings had already left for school, but Laura was not old enough to join them. Her younger brothers were still outside. She hadn't seen her father that morning, but that wasn't unusual. He was probably out in the fields or in his workshop, repairing a piece of farm equipment. She decided to take a bath. The house was quiet, and she enjoyed having the bathroom to herself for a change.

After her bath, she returned to the large bedroom she shared with three of her sisters and dressed in her usual old jeans and shirt. Just as she was about to leave the room, Laura noticed her new Sunday dress hanging in the closet. Laura didn't have many clothes. She was much smaller and skinnier than her next older sister, Julie, and couldn't wear the usual hand-me-downs. New dresses were rarer still. She had only two other good dresses, and both were getting old and worn. That new pink dress with its puffy sleeves, narrow waist, and wide, pleated skirt gleamed on the hanger like a beautiful jewel. Laura could hardly wait until Sunday when she could wear it to Mass.

Then she thought, *There's nobody here to see me. I could try it on!* Quickly, she stripped off her everyday clothes. She carefully lifted the beautiful dress down from its hanger and slipped it over her head. The soft folds settled around her, and she patted the skirt down and buttoned up the little buttons on the front of the dress. Then she had another thought: *I'll just eat breakfast in this dress. Nobody will ever know.* She put on her Sunday shoes and skipped into the kitchen, feeling like a princess.

Laura was still seated on the bench at the table when her father entered the kitchen. Laura looked up at him fearfully. Would he punish her for wearing the pink dress?

Her dad said nothing, just stood there by the door and looked at Laura. Then, without saying a word, he walked over to the table and reached for her hand. Laura obediently put her hand in her father's and followed him out of the kitchen. *What's Dad going to do?* Laura thought. *Is he going to punish me?* Her father led her down the hallway to a bedroom. It wasn't her bedroom, and it wasn't the room her father shared with her mother. Rather, it was the bare, unadorned bedroom where all four of her brothers slept in two big double beds.

Why are we going in here? Laura was puzzled.

"Lie down on the bed, Laura," her father said. Laura did as she was told, nervously smoothing her skirt with both hands. Her father reached out with his right hand and flipped the pink skirt up over her head so that she couldn't see. "Turn over," he said; his voice sounded odd and tight. Laura obeyed. The pink skirt still covered her head.

Laura felt the bed creak under her father's considerable weight. Then, through her panties, she felt something hard being rubbed back and forth along the cleft between her buttocks. After a while, the bed creaked again, and she heard her father stand up. After a moment, he said, "I'm finished, Laura. You can go now." And he left.

Left alone on the bed, Laura stared at the ceiling, dry eyed and shaking. *What just happened to me? Why did this happen to me?* She didn't know what had happened, but instinctively she knew it was wrong and bad. But her father had done it to her, and her father was good. So *she* must be the bad one. She must be full of badness for this to have happened to her.

She wanted to tell someone about it, but she knew that she must never say a word. She was young, but she already knew that there were some things that nobody in the family ever talked about. But more important, it would be terrible for her if anyone found out how bad she was. She would have to keep it a secret. She would never speak of it. She would try her best to forget it.

The bond of trust between father and daughter was broken. She vowed that she would stay as far away from her father as possible. *I will run*, she thought. *When he comes near me again, I will run as fast as I can.* Running became Laura's coping mechanism, and in time, she would become a very fast runner.

Laura got up off the bed and quickly took off the pink dress. Why had she ever thought it was pretty? It was an ugly dress! Ugly! Ugly! *Ugly!* She hated the dress from that day forward, even though she had to wear it to church on many Sundays. She remembered that her mother had told her several times that her father was disappointed when she was born because she was a girl. Did this bad thing happen because she was a girl? From that time on and for many years to come, she disliked being a girl. And she hated the color pink for the rest of her life.

Laura prayed to God, her special Friend. *Why did You let this happen to me?* But for the first time, Laura didn't sense God's presence or that He was listening to her prayers. It was the beginning of the end of her childish, unquestioning faith in God.

Life changed that day for Laura. She was no longer carefree, innocent, and happy. She began to struggle with a general sense of sadness and became more aware of what was going on in her home. She realized for the first time that her mother and father often fought. There were frequent loud, angry shouting matches between them.

Her parents' worst arguments were usually over money. While Emmett was good at managing the farm, he was not responsible with money, often making rash decisions to buy things that kept the family in debt and without money for necessities. He hated that Mary had to work. It contributed to his own sense of failure. He had no tools to deal with conflict, and irrationally, he took his anger out on his wife and children.

His stress level rose to impossible heights, and his health and his family suffered. Mary was a strong-willed woman who refused to accept meekly whatever her husband said. She argued back, standing her ground. Many times the arguments were about finances, but just as often, they were about pointless things, such as who owned the tree in the front yard. From there, a pointless argument would escalate into a physical confrontation. Laura watched as her dad would raise his arm to hit her mother, and her mother would put up both arms to protect her head and defend herself from being beaten.

Laura began to realize that her father often hit her mother, smacking her, slapping her, striking her with whatever was at hand, and shoving her around. Laura became aware of what her older siblings already knew: their father was a violent, irrationally angry man, and no one, certainly not Laura or her little brothers, was safe from him. Fear was a constant companion in the Sicking household.

The beatings were the worst part of life for the children. They came often, and they were brutal. No child was safe, although some were beaten more often and more viciously than others. The children never knew when their father's wrath would be unleashed. He called it discipline, but many times there was neither rhyme nor reason to it. Infractions that were ignored one day led to severe punishment the next. One child's misbehavior was ignored, and another's was severely punished. The beatings would start off as spankings, but then Emmett Sicking's anger would escalate out of control.

Verbal abuse was also constant. Mary and the children received the brunt of a steady stream of belittling, cursing, and name-calling. This added to Laura's inner feelings of her own badness. The children banded together in cliques, based on age and birth order, in an effort to protect each other and their mother. If someone did something wrong, the other children would conceal that information from their father. Silence and secrecy were the order of the day—every day.

In general, there were no close relationships among the children, except for Virginia and Deb and Laura and Bill. Often, modeling what they knew, the children resorted to hitting each other when disputes arose. One day Laura got angry with Bill, her best buddy among her siblings, and before she knew what was happening, she was beating him—striking him repeatedly. Poor Bill fell to the ground, covering his head with his arms, warding off his big sister's furious blows.

Laura was appalled when she came to her senses and realized what she had done. *Why did I do that? I love Bill! I lost control, just like my father.* Her sense of her own wickedness and self-hatred was amplified by this event. No amount of rosaries, penances, or lighting of candles could ever tip the balance in her favor. She promised herself never to hit another human being again, and she never did.

Their father turned his anger on Mark and Joyce more than the other kids. Laura didn't know why they were treated worse than the others. It wasn't clear what made the difference. Virginia was the only one who was able to cry big crocodile tears as soon as their father raised his hand to strike her, and that seemed to keep him from hitting her. She was the lucky one.

Joyce got it the worst of anybody. Whether it was her resemblance to himself or her feistiness, their father's anger toward her often turned violent. Joyce often turned her own temper on her siblings, causing bad feelings that left her without protection from them when her dad beat her.

For Laura and Bryan, although they were beaten themselves, the anguish of seeing their brother Mark getting beaten more viciously and frequently was almost more than they could bear. Mark was a tender, sensitive soul—quiet and introverted. Bryan was a spitfire, as feisty as Laura and smart as a whip. Bryan and Laura determined that they would stick together to protect Mark from their father's anger. They even tried negotiating with him.

"Dad, you have to promise us something," Laura pleaded once as her dad was about to spank Mark. Their father looked up; his hand holding a flat wooden paddle was already raised over Mark, who was bent over his father's knees.

"Promise you what?"

"Dad," Bryan chimed in, "you have to promise us that you will only spank Mark ten times and no more."

Their father nodded distractedly. "OK, OK," he replied. Then he began Mark's spanking, Laura and Bryan counting each swat out loud. But when he got to ten, he kept right on going—his temper rising and the force of the beating growing stronger with each stroke. No amount of negotiation ever stopped the abuse.

No matter how bad it was to be beaten, the real torture was to watch help-lessly while a sibling was being hit and being unable to stop it. Bryan and Laura tried distracting their father by making faces, sticking out their tongues, and putting their thumbs in their ears. Their dad got up and ran after them, leaving Mark to slip away from his grasp.

The children learned to run fast. They dived under beds when their father chased them. They listened for his footsteps on the wooden floors, learning to judge by the sound whether he was enraged or not. They took the screens off their bedroom windows, so they could jump out into the bushes to escape him. They kept the doors unlocked and open at all times so that they could run out of the house.

Bill, the youngest, didn't come into the house. An outdoorsman from a very young age, he spent all of his spare time in the woods and fields when he wasn't doing his chores. It was his escape. Because he was outside so often, he was not aware of the magnitude of the conflict that was occurring.

What was even worse for the children than being beaten themselves was seeing their mother being repeatedly and cruelly hit. The kids, especially Mark, Bryan, and Laura, tried their hardest to defend their mother. They linked arms and used their bodies to form a barrier between their mom and their dad. This interference only made their dad more annoyed and his verbal abuse more malicious, but at least he turned away and did not hit their mom when the children got between them.

Mary's working days were long and hard. She rose before anybody else, first waking Laura and Bill at 4:00 A.M. and then preparing breakfast for the family before leaving for her job. Laura and the other children saw very little of their mother. With such a demanding schedule, there wasn't a lot of time for her to spend with the children. When their mother wasn't available, Joan became the substitute mom to all the children.

Mary was a beautiful woman with dark, curly hair and a fine olive com-plexion. Despite having given birth to so many children, she was strong and physically fit. She was also an expert seamstress. She was paid by the piece at the sewing factory, and by pushing herself hard, she made decent money for a common female laborer. When she came home in the evening, however, she was exhausted. When Mary was tired, she could have a very sharp tongue; on occasion, Laura felt its effects.

When she misbehaved, her mother would say, "I bought you at Sears for twenty-five dollars. If you can't behave yourself, I'll take you back to the store and get my money back!" Laura's young heart sank. Would she really take her back for a refund? She imagined herself as a sad little girl, who was returned for a refund, standing among the appliances and lawn mowers at Sears—traded in for twenty-five dollars.

The older girls regularly prepared the evening meal and did the dishes. The family had dinner together, and afterward the parents watched the news on television, then went to bed, spending little time with the children.

Laura desperately longed for her mother to love and value her, but she felt that she never really knew her. Competing with ten other siblings for a mother's attention was hard enough for any child, without the added demands that existed in the Sicking house.

One evening after dinner, Laura was passing her parents' room. The door was open, and her mother was lying on the bed with her eyes closed.

"Mom, are you asleep?" Laura asked, hardly able to believe that she might actually have her mother to herself.

"Come in, Laura, and talk to me for a minute. I'm not asleep."

Laura spent the next few minutes telling her mother about school. Mary talked a little about her job and what she did at the factory. At that moment, Laura's mom was loving and kind. Laura was chattering away when her mom interrupted her.

"Laura, I'm dog tired. Let me go to sleep now."

The few quiet moments that they spent together would be a memory Laura would cherish all of her life.

CHAPTER 3

....

"Mother Mary Is There for You, Children!"

Laura was seven when she started first grade at the Sacred Heart Catholic School in Muenster. All of the kids in the family, including Laura, looked forward to going to school. The chores at home didn't diminish and their days became even longer, but at least school provided some respite from the wretchedness of their home life.

Laura was excited the first day she climbed up the stone steps to the big double doors of the brick school. She felt all grown up. She loved her new school uniform—a white shirt and a blue skirt with a bib in the front and two wide straps that crisscrossed in the back. Her sister Joan, an excellent seamstress, had made it for her. All of the girls in the school wore one just like it, and it made Laura feel as though she really belonged.

Laura was grateful for Joan's kindness. She was a really great big sister! In many ways, Joan, the oldest of the eleven children, became the mother Laura's own mother wasn't able to be. Joan was a natural leader—smart, strong, capable, kind, and honest. The kids looked up to her and respected her judgment. Plump, with dark, curly hair like their mother, Joan was always calm and serene. She never got angry and never overreacted. The balance she brought to the household stood in stark contrast to their parents' erratic behavior.

Joan had taught herself to sew when she was only eleven. To Laura, that handmade blue-and-white uniform was a symbol of her sister's goodness. In Laura's eyes, Joan was an example of what a good woman should be. Laura admired her and wanted to be like her.

Laura also admired her first-grade teacher, Sister Genevieve, who looked a little like a rotund angel in her white habit and black-edged veil, with a large wooden crucifix on a chain around her neck. She was round faced and rosy cheeked, and her voice was soft and sweet. She was loving and friendly to all of the children.

Laura wanted to be just like her; but at seven, she was skinny and wiry and lively and mischievous. Her short, white-blond curls were always in wild disarray. Laura hated those curls. She longed for long, dark straight hair.

Laura loved Sister Genevieve; when Sister gave each child a rosary and began to teach them how to pray, Laura listened attentively. She already knew about prayer. Prayer was talking to God, and God had been her Friend for as long as she could remember.

Her mother had a rosary, and on special days, such as Easter, she prayed the rosary with the children. Sister explained that the rosary was meant to help people pray. People started by saying a prayer, then they moved their fingers to the large bead next to the cross, and they said another prayer. They kept going, around the sixty beads on the rosary, saying a prayer for each bead.

Then Sister Genevieve said something shocking: there were special prayers that were the only ones people should pray, and God wanted people to memorize them exactly and say them over and over again. That's what the beads were for, to help people keep track of how many times they said each of the prayers. Laura realized that she was praying all wrong!

She resolved that she would not pray those baby prayers she had been praying. God was too busy to listen to a little girl's wants and needs. He wanted to hear grown-up prayers. So Laura memorized her Our Fathers, Hail Marys, and Glory Bes and started praying with the rosary for an hour or more a day. She carried her rosary with her and prayed while she did her chores. She was determined to be a good Catholic. The close connection she felt with God as she talked to Him as her best Friend was gradually slipping away, and she lost a little more of her childlike faith in a loving, personal heavenly Father who cared for her.

Perhaps other children got something different from Catholic school, but in Laura's impressionable mind, what she learned from Sister Genevieve's gentle teaching was that God the Father was a very busy Man. Children shouldn't bother Him with their insignificant requests—God didn't have time for such things. There were a lot of things to take care of in the universe—big important things. Jesus was very busy too.

But Mary, the mother of Jesus? "Mary is different," Sister said. "Mother Mary is there for you, children. Pray to Mary! Bring all your wants and needs to her, and she will help you."

In a strange way, this made perfect sense to Laura. In her family, she knew her father was a smart man, and he was in charge, but he was very busy too.

It was her mother or her big sister Joan that Laura went to when she needed something. But she longed to spend time with and bond with her mother. Her mother, though, was often tired and burdened down with problems of her own and with her demanding schedule. Her mom could be strict; nobody doubted that. She would wash the children's mouths out with soap if she heard them say a curse word, but she never, ever hit anybody.

Laura was soon praying to Mary for help with the little problems she encountered at home and at school. Later on in Catholic school, she was instructed to pray to other saints, but Mary remained the most important. For the big problems, such as protection from her father's wrath, she still secretly prayed directly to God the Father but felt guilty as she did so. She hoped He could spare a few minutes away from directing the universe when she really needed Him. As time went by, however, and nothing changed at home, Laura became angry with God for doing nothing to stop what was happening to her. She prayed over and over again, waiting for an answer that didn't come.

The children at Sacred Heart Catholic School started every morning with Mass. Nothing was required of the children except that they sit quietly and follow along in their missals, chanting the responses at the appropriate times.

Girls were required to cover their heads for Mass. Most of the girls wore small beanie caps. If a girl forgot her beanie, Sister Genevieve would slap a square of lace on her head. Females were not allowed to be in church without covering their heads.

One day one of the other girls in Laura's class told her, "Hey, Laura, I heard that if you cut all your hair off, it'll grow back in straight."

"Really? That would be great!"

"Yeah, my mom knows somebody who had curly hair, and she shaved it all off. Sure enough, it grew back in straight!"

Laura couldn't wait to get home from school that day. She made a beeline for her father's bathroom and found his shaving kit. She lathered up his shaving brush and carefully painted her head with the lather. Looking in the mirror over his sink, she shaved off all the hair she could see. She was holding a hand mirror and awkwardly reaching for the back of her head with the razor, when her mother came into the bathroom.

"Laura! What are you doing?"

"I'm going to have straight hair! A kid in my class told me that if I shave it all off, it will come back in straight."

"Laura, that's just not true!" Her mother shook her head, looking distressed and annoyed. Then she got the scissors, and without another word, evened up the back of her little girl's hair as much as she could.

Somehow, in her excitement about having long, straight hair, Laura hadn't thought about what it would be like to face the world with a shorn head. She wore her beanie all day, every day, for several long months. Sure enough, when her hair grew back in, it was still blond and curly.

Things changed for Laura in second grade. Not only did she lose her two front teeth, like many of the kids in her class, but she got a new teacher. Sister Aloysia was tall and slim, with a long, solemn, unsmiling face and stern gray eyes. She always carried a ruler in her right hand, and she slammed that ruler down on the children's hands if they misbehaved.

Sister Aloysia thought that Laura talked too much. Laura was outgoing and friendly and talked with the other kids when she shouldn't have. She often felt the sting of Sister Aloysia's ruler. Naturally, Laura disliked and feared the nun. She didn't need another person in her life who hit her.

One day Sister Aloysia's patience was pushed to the breaking point. "I have a spanking machine in the closet for bad boys and girls," she spoke sharply to Laura in her low voice. "If you continue to be bad and talk too much, I'm going to put you in the spanking machine, and it will spank you until it gets all the badness out of you!"

Laura stared openmouthed at her teacher. She believed Sister Aloysia. She thought about her life at home. She thought about the beatings she and her siblings endured and the bad things her father said. She thought about the bad thing that her father did when she wore the pink dress.

From that point on, Laura never spoke out of turn in class. *I would die in that spanking machine,* she thought, and her young heart sank. *There is so much badness in me; no machine could ever get it out.*

Laura redoubled her efforts to get rid of the wickedness by trying to be good. She would be the best Catholic child. She embraced her mother's wish that she would become a nun and never get married.

Always a little sponge, she absorbed other ideas from Catholic school and from her mother at home: Catholicism was the one true faith and all other religions were false; Protestants were evil and were going to hell; the Catholic Church would one day form a one-world government and a one-world church, with the pope at its head; and the Bible was not meant for regular people like her to read.

She learned in school that there were three kinds of sins. Mortal sins were terrible things, such as murder. Venial sins were smaller things, such as talking too much in class or telling a lie. These categories required confession and penance. There was a third category of sins that the sisters called white sins. These were things that were wrong but which people did to help somebody, such as telling a friend she looked pretty when one really didn't think so. They didn't require penance. Because of the nuns' teachings in class, Laura developed the belief that God would strike her dead if she ever missed Mass.

Laura developed a system of keeping score—balancing her sins against her penances and good deeds. She wrote down her bad and good deeds with points for each in a book. She got in the positive by going to Mass and confession, saying rosaries, and lighting candles.

Laura's fierce dedication to Catholicism had nothing to do with a love for God. It was her "medication" against the badness she felt. She became fanatical about keeping score and doing her best to get rid of the sins. She would do this consistently for the next seven years.

By third grade, things changed again. Sacred Heart Catholic School raised its tuition to more than double what it was the previous year. Big families such as Laura's could no longer afford to send all of their children to Sacred Heart. Joan, who was sixteen that year, had a job in the Catholic school's cafeteria that helped to pay the tuition for some of the Sicking kids, but others, including Laura, had to leave.

In fact, there was a mass exodus that year to the town's small public school just across the street. Laura, along with about fifty other Catholic kids, joined the school's twelve Protestant kids in the third grade, and immediately, changes began to happen at Muenster Elementary School.

The kids were excused each morning to go to Mass. Catholic prayers replaced Protestant prayers in the public school. Some of the Protestant kids rebelled, refusing to pray the Catholic rote prayers or to go to Mass, resulting in fights between the kids of the two schools.

For Laura, the changes went deeper. New friends brought new ideas into her life. Mary Anne, for instance, was a Bible-believing Baptist and well versed in the Scriptures, and she made Laura her personal evangelism project.

At the third-grade Easter party, the classroom was decorated with bunnies and Easter eggs. Mary Anne said to Laura, "Laura, did you know that the Easter bunny and Easter eggs have nothing to do with Jesus dying on the cross?"

"Yes, they do!" replied Laura.

"Well, how?" Mary Anne's freckled face was now only inches from Laura's.

"Um, I don't know, but I'll tell you tomorrow," Laura replied.

Laura's mother told her that she should take any questions about religion to the family's priest. The priest was a tall, slender, dark-haired man, and he was always kind to the children. He had an office in the Sacred Heart Catholic School, so Laura walked across the street to see him after class. He welcomed her warmly.

"Father, I know that Easter is about Christ's death and resurrection, but how is the Easter bunny connected with Jesus dying on the cross?"

"Well, Laura," the priest replied, all smiles. "You know how bunny rabbits are cute and soft—all furry and cuddly?"

"Yeah."

"Well, child, that's how Jesus is."

Laura thanked the priest politely and left his office, thinking, *That's the stupidest answer I've ever heard.* It was so stupid that Laura told Mary Anne she was right: bunny rabbits and Easter eggs had nothing to do with Jesus dying on the cross.

Sensing success, Mary Anne continued. "You Catholics think getting baptized by sprinkling is what the Bible says, but that's not right. It says you're supposed to be dunked."

"Really?" Laura was not as inclined to argue with her friend because Mary Anne was right the last time. She was curious, however, so she went back to the priest and asked him. "Did people used to get baptized by being dunked under the water?"

"Yes, child, a long time ago the early Christian church baptized everybody by immersion, or dunking, as you call it. They didn't do sprinkling. That's something that the church changed later."

"But, Father, why did we change it? Shouldn't we do it the way the early Christians did?"

"No child, we don't need to do it that way anymore. Sprinkling is just fine. We changed it because, if you got all the way dunked, you would get wet. Then you might get a cold, and who knows, you might get sick and die! You don't want to get sick and die, do you, Laura?" the priest smiled. Obviously, the case was closed.

This time Laura left the priest's office confident that the priest had a good explanation.

His answer made sense to her. She didn't like getting wet!

The next day Laura told Mary Anne what the priest said about baptism, and her friend had no reply. But she was soon back with a new bit of information. "Laura, the Bible says Jesus had brothers and sisters."

"No! He did not!" Laura was sure she was on solid ground with this one.

"Did too!" shot back Mary Anne.

Laura did not reply, but this time she went to her mother with Mary Anne's latest assertion. Her mother ignored her question and went right to the heart of the matter.

"Laura, that girl is a Protestant," her mom said, closing her hand over Laura's skinny arm so hard that it hurt. "You should have nothing to do with her. She is not your friend. Stay away from her."

Laura knew that her mother's loathing of Protestants ran almost as deep as her love of the Catholic Church. Mary was ten years old in 1939 when Hitler invaded Poland and World War II began. She and her family were members of a German-speaking Catholic Church in their small town of Scotland, Texas. Mary loved and respected her church and her German-speaking priest.

At that time, there were racial attacks against German-speaking immigrants, and sometimes they turned deadly. One night members of the Ku Klux Klan tarred and feathered her Catholic priest because it was alleged that he supported the Germans.

As a child, listening during church services, she heard updates on his medical condition, which filled her with sadness and pain. The priest died after a long hospitalization. Mary viewed this horrible act of violence as the evil work of Protestants, and it instilled in her a deep hatred for them for the rest of her life. The actual facts of the story became obscured over time, but the hatred for Protestants remained vivid and alive in her heart.

OK, Laura thought. *Mom's right. Mary Anne is not my friend. I just won't talk to her anymore.* And she didn't. Imagine Laura's surprise many years later when she read in the Bible about Jesus having both brothers and sisters! Mary Anne was right.

CHAPTER 4

....

"Who Broke Mom's Blue Vase?"

Despite occasionally being required to stay home from school to work on the farm, Laura made pretty decent grades. This wasn't due to parental encouragement. Her father frequently called the children stupid. In fact, her parents were indifferent to grades. They would stack up the kids' report cards in a pile and sign them, barely looking at their marks. With the many hours spent each day on farm chores, there was no time for homework or study. Homework, if it got done at all, happened at school during recess or the lunch hour.

There was a television in the Sicking home; but if the children were caught in front of the television, it indicated they didn't have enough work to do—and they got more work. They watched television only when their parents orchestrated it.

Laura, as the youngest girl, was still the one sent out to wake the cows in the mornings. One Sunday morning when she was about ten, she went out alone to wake the cows at four in the morning. The cows were in a nearby pasture, so she was walking rather than driving the truck. The family owned a two thousand–pound Brahman bull named Tromper—called that because of the way he made the ground shake when he walked. Tromper was powerful and dangerous, and most of the time he was kept locked up, but sometimes he got out. He had chased Laura on a couple of occasions, but she had been able to run and dive under the fence before he caught up to her. As she walked among the cows that Sunday morning, shouting as usual, suddenly Tromper loomed up out of the darkness, running at full speed and heading straight for her. She looked around wildly. The fence was too far away. Her only possible choice was to climb the closest elm tree on the edge of the woods, which she did, scrambling out of Tromper's reach just as he reached the base of the tree. There she sat, shaking in the dark, as Tromper snorted and pawed the ground under the tree.

Laura sat in the tree for six hours, with the huge bull just a few feet below her the entire time. The cows wandered into the milking barn without her, just a little later than usual. Bill was her milking partner as usual, but he didn't say anything that might get Laura in trouble; he just did her share of the work. Nobody else noticed that Laura hadn't come back from waking the cows.

When it was time to leave for Mass that morning, their mother looked around. "Where's Laura? Why isn't she ready to go to church?" The kids didn't know. Eventually, somebody figured out that their youngest sister never returned from waking the cows, and they found her, still sitting, cramped and cold, up in an elm tree. They had to use the truck to scare Tromper away from the base of the elm tree in order to rescue Laura.

Things lightened up a little around the Sicking household at Christmastime. The children looked forward to playing games in their free time during the school holiday. They loved games. The kids received an allowance of four dollars a month. They were expected to buy their own clothes, shoes, school supplies, and other necessities out of this money, leaving very little for anything else. If they were very frugal, they could occasionally buy a toy or a game.

During the Christmas that Laura was nine, Cliff and Joyce, who were sixteen and fifteen, pooled their savings and bought a Ouija board.

Cliff opened the box, and it contained a large, peculiar-looking brown board and a little triangular-shaped object. The board was printed with the letters of the alphabet in two half-circles, with the numbers one through nine in a straight line beneath them. The words *No* and *Yes* were printed in black on the upper right and left corners, and at the bottom was the word *Good-bye.*

Cliff read out the directions, which specified that two people were to sit on either side of the board with their knees touching. Naturally, Cliff and Joyce were the kids who would play because they owned the game, so they sat down across from each other at the table and the other kids crowded around to watch.

The directions said each person was to place one finger on the triangle, called a planchette. Then the idea was to ask the board questions, and the triangle was supposed to move to the letters and spell out an answer. This looked like fun! Cliff and Joyce put their fingers on the planchette. Everyone was quiet. Joyce started by asking, "Whose report card has six As?" They watched, fascinated, as the little triangle began to move. J-O-A-N, it spelled out. Well, that was the right answer, but it was no surprise. Everybody knew Joan made the best grades.

"That question was too easy," said Lois. "We need to ask it something harder."

"What shall we ask it?" Cliff looked up at his siblings.

"How many bushels of seed does it take to plant the wheat field?" somebody said.

"We don't even know the answer to that!" Joyce said.

"Yeah, but Dad does." So Joyce directed the question to the board.

The triangle moved again, spelling out "2-0-0." Mark immediately ran to ask their dad. He said, "Two hundred bushels!" which Mark reported back to the waiting group of kids. That was amazing, because only their dad knew the right answer to the question. But the kids were still not convinced about this game. Everyone tried to think of a very hard question that no one knew the answer to. Then somebody suggested that they ask, "Who broke Mom's blue vase?" This was an unsolved mystery in the household—something nobody had admitted. The planchette started to move again. Once again the kids leaned in for a better view. M-A-R-K, it spelled.

"Yeah," the culprit owned up, looking startled. "It was me. How did you know that?"

"What?" Both Cliff and Joyce spoke at the same time. "We didn't know!"

"Sure you did! You moved that thing."

"I didn't move it. It must have been Cliff!" Joyce exclaimed. "It wasn't me! You must have moved it!"

The kids began to argue over who was moving the planchette. Half of the children were sure it was Cliff, and the other half thought it was Joyce.

Then someone said, "Ask the board who is moving it." Everyone stopped arguing. That was a great idea, and Joyce asked, "Who is moving the planchette?"

She and Cliff put their fingers on the planchette again, and it began to move. It spelled out I A-M.

"Who are you?" Joyce asked.

The planchette moved. M-Y N-A-M-E I-S L-U-C-I-F-E-R. It stopped. Then it began to move again. This time it spelled out S-A-T-A-N. Moving faster and faster, it spelled out T-H-E D-E-V-I-L, A-P-O-L-L-Y-O-N, and A-B-A-D-D-O-N. The children had never heard of the last two names, but the first three were familiar enough. This was getting scary! Laura felt the hair stand up on the back of her neck. She stepped back from the table, shaking with fear. This was no ordinary game. She didn't know what it was, but it was probably not a good thing to play with.

Cliff and Joyce persisted. "Who do you like here?" Joyce asked. The board spelled out I H-A-T-E E-V-E-R-Y-O-N-E E-X-C-E-P-T J-O-Y-C-E. I L-I-K-E J-O-Y-C-E.

That was enough, even for Cliff and Joyce. They put the board away. Even though she was just a child, Laura sensed the presence of something evil.

Fifteen years later Laura would read Revelation 9:11, "And they had a king over them, which is the angel of the bottomless pit, whose name in the Hebrew tongue is Abaddon, but in the Greek tongue hath his name Apollyon" (KJV).

There were those two names for Satan that the Ouija board had spelled out long ago. Laura felt the same conviction she had known as a child the night Cliff and Joyce brought the Ouija board home. She believed the devil was real and that he knew a lot of things.

CHAPTER 5

············

"Please Don't Leave Us!"

The beatings at home became so bad by the time Laura was ten that she prayed often that God would cause her father to die. For years, her older siblings talked about ways to kill their father. She desperately wanted that to happen so that the pain would stop, but it never did.

Whenever their father was out of earshot, the children begged their mother to leave him. "Mom, we have to get away from Dad. We *have* to! Let's just pack up the car and go. Please, Mom! We can't live like this. We can't take it anymore!"

"Please, Mom!" One of the older girls would pick up the plea. "We can make it on our own! We girls can go to work. We're old enough to get waitressing jobs. We can bring in some money. We can do it, Mom! We'll do anything!" This begging was always done in whispers.

Mary Sicking looked at her desperate brood. Joan and Cliff were nearly old enough to be on their own, if they needed to be, but there were six daughters and three little boys who still needed her support.

God knew she wanted to leave! Once, after a particularly bad beating, she just disappeared, leaving both her husband and her children to fend for themselves. Joan had to hunt her down. That wasn't too hard because Mary Sicking had fled to her own parents' home.

However, she thought about leaving often—even dreamed about it. Just thinking about the possibility of freeing herself and her children from her husband's beatings and constant verbal abuse lifted her heart. But how could she afford it?

Divorce was unthinkable. The church said it was a sin. But a separation might be possible.

She decided to ask Muenster's only attorney about getting a separation. She made an appointment to see him. The lawyer listened as Mary Sicking described the horrific treatment she and her children endured.

"Well, you're in a difficult situation, aren't you, Mrs. Sicking? Tell me, do you know whose name is on the deed to your farm and your house? Whose name is on your car title? And is your savings account joint, or is it in your husband's name only?"

"I'm not sure," Mary replied hesitantly. "My husband has always taken care of all of those things."

The lawyer smiled a tired, knowing smile. "You come back when you know the answers to those questions, ma'am, and we'll talk again."

Mary learned that everything—the land, the house, the car, and the savings account—was in Emmett Sicking's name. Absolutely nothing belonged to her. The lawyer advised her that only a formal divorce would require her husband to divide their assets. She thought that without a share of the assets, she would be unable to support her children. A separation was out of the question.

Mary received this news quietly, digesting the information the lawyer gave her. Was she strong enough to take the only option remaining to her—divorce? Then the lawyer said something that shattered that idea too.

"Mrs. Sicking, as your attorney, I must advise you that if you and your husband were to divorce, and he was to ask the court for custody of his sons, the laws of this state would be on his side. It is quite likely that a judge would grant you custody of your daughters, but your three youngest sons would most definitely have to remain with their father. The law would recognize that he requires the boys' help on the farm."

Their mother drove home with a heavy heart that day. She gathered the kids together as soon as there was an opportunity and told them what the lawyer had said. The girls didn't care about the division of assets. They were sure they could find jobs and help with the expenses. They knew they could make it work. They pleaded with her to just leave.

They could see, however, that their mother was very concerned about leaving the three youngest boys behind. She saw the fear and dread on Bryan's, Mark's, and Bill's faces when they heard what the lawyer had said.

"Mom, if you leave, we don't know how we are going to make it!" Mark said as his voice filled with anxiety.

"Yeah, Mom!" Bryan added. "We can't face him alone. Please don't leave us!" Their mother's face reflected the desperation she saw on her sons' faces. There were no tears. This family's pain was beyond tears. How could she possibly abandon these three young boys? They were nine, eight, and seven years old.

The girls still begged her to go; their pleading was equal to the boys.

Mary Sicking had two choices, and they were both terrible: She could leave the boys behind and take the girls with her, removing them from their father's beatings and abuse, or she could remain in the home, continuing to expose all of her children and herself to a life of misery, while providing what little protection and support her presence afforded.

Their mother promised the children that she would make a decision soon. She thought it over for several days, and then she called the girls aside, one by one, and attempted to explain to them why she was going to stay.

"I have no college degree," she said. "I can't get the kind of job I would need. There is no way I could possibly make enough money to support us, even with your help."

Then Mary laid out her carefully thought-out strategy and explained it to each of her daughters. First, she urged each girl to go to college. "I want you to have a good education," she told them. "I want you to be able to earn a good living. If you have to leave your husband someday, I want you to be able to take your children with you and not be stuck the way I am."

Although their mother's plan offered no comfort for the present, the girls would eventually take her advice about education to heart. All seven daughters would obtain college degrees, and some would get several advanced degrees. They would become high-earning, successful career women. Indeed, some of them would become wealthy. The boys were not similarly encouraged to get an education, and none of them did—with the exception of Bill, whose employer was legally required to send him to college after he broke his back at work.

Mary's plan for her daughters also extended to teaching them to be good money managers, and she began to take a more active role in handling the family's finances. She also started a practice of putting the oldest daughter who was still at home in charge of paying the bills, beginning with Joyce, who was seventeen. So Joyce's name was added to the family checking account.

The second part of Mary's strategy involved herself. She started socking money away. She quit her job at the sewing factory and took a better-paying position as a cook in the Muenster Memorial Hospital. Always frugal and strong-willed, she focused her efforts on becoming financially independent. She eventually accumulated a considerable personal fortune of her own, even though she never earned more than $8.75 an hour at any of the places where she worked.

Mary also talked to the boys after she made the decision not to leave their father. She explained that she was staying with their father both because she couldn't afford to leave and in order to protect them.

The decision to stay in her marriage was one of the most important choices of Mary Sicking's life. Laura, like her sisters, disagreed with it at the time; but when Laura became an adult, she realized the strength of character that decision required and came to respect her mother for making it.

That event marked another milestone in Laura's life. There would be no reprieve from the abuse she and her siblings endured. It would continue. Her mother's decision to stay set the stage for what happened next.

CHAPTER 6

....

"We Have to Kill Dad!"

Mary's new job came with medical insurance. This was helpful since Emmett Sicking had another schizophrenic episode when Laura was about twelve and a half years old. This time he asked to be committed and was sent to a mental hospital about an hour away in Sherman, Texas. He stayed there for four months during the summer of 1969. It was a season of peace and healing for his family.

On their first visit to their father in the hospital, the children noticed that he had lost a lot of weight. "Did you bring me any candy?" was their dad's first question after a hello.

"What?"

"Did you bring any candy? I really want some candy."

Mary spoke up. "No, Emmett, we didn't bring any candy. Don't they give you desserts?"

"Yeah, but only for lunch and dinner. And they only let me eat three times a day." Their father was not happy about the regulation of his eating habits and was desperate for sweets. "I need candy! Next time, be sure you bring candy!" he insisted.

When Laura was nineteen, her father's doctors diagnosed her father's medical problem as untreated, out-of-control diabetes. She wondered at the time if it was possible that he had had diabetes for those many years and not schizophrenia. She found it impossible not to blame the doctors and nurses who overlooked his diabetes when he was under their care during his three stays in mental hospitals. It was apparent, even to twelve-year-old Laura, that there was something very wrong about her father's uncontrollable craving for sweets.

It was fall when Emmett finally returned home. He appeared to be a changed man. He seemed healthy and cheerful and had lost more than 100 pounds. His family welcomed him home; for a short time, life was enjoyable, and the farmhouse was filled with cautious hope. But their happiness was short lived. Emmett reverted almost at once to his old eating habits, living on Twinkies washed down with soda. Soon he was feeling bad again. He went from agreeable and peaceable to irritable and violent in a matter of weeks, and life was back to its old miserable pattern. Within a few months, he regained all the weight.

On a hot day in the summer of the following year, Emmett had an episode that Laura would later recognize as diabetic shock. He and the kids were baling hay. This was a big operation on the ranch and required the whole family to work as a team. One of the children drove the tractor, towing a hay baler and trailer. The baler collected the hay, formed it into rectangular bales, and dumped them into the trailer. Two kids in the trailer stacked the forty-pound bales as they came off the baler. Once the trailer was full of hay, it was attached to the pickup truck. Then their dad drove the truck to the barn where the trailer was unhitched and left for two kids to unload the hay and stack it in the barn. Two girls remained in the house, preparing food for lunch.

On that day, Laura was assigned to ride in the pickup truck with her father as they pulled the full trailers from the field to the barn and the empty ones back again. Her job was to hook up the trailers behind the pickup and open or close the gates as needed.

Emmett, as usual, was drinking Cokes and eating Twinkies constantly, with a stash of both beside him. The field they were working in produced a very abundant crop of hay that summer, and the bales were coming faster than usual, forcing everyone, even their dad, to step up the pace. It was hot, frantic work, and everyone struggled to keep up with their part of the process.

No one had time to replenish Emmett's stash, and he was without his snacks for a couple of hours. Laura was behind the pickup, hooking up a trailer full of hay, when she heard him yell. "Laura, quick, get in the truck, now!" he screamed.

Laura dropped the trailer hitch and climbed into the pickup. One look at her father, and she knew something was terribly wrong. His whole body was shaking violently. His face was chalk white, and huge amounts of sweat were pouring off him. Laura was terrified. She had seen her father in some extreme situations, but she had never seen him like this.

"I've got to have a Coke and a Twinkie," he gasped. "Now!" Somehow he managed to drive the truck back to the house, and Laura ran inside and got him what he needed.

"Here, Dad," she said, placing the Coke and a Twinkie into his trembling hands. She watched him drink the Coke in a few swallows and devour the

Twinkie, and in less than a minute, the shaking stopped, the sweating subsided, and the color returned to his face.

"I'm fine now," her dad said, as though nothing had happened. He started up the truck, and they headed back out to the field.

What was that? Laura thought. *There is something really bad going on here.* She remembered the time in the hospital, less than a year before, when her father begged for candy like an alcoholic or a drug addict. *Something is really wrong with Dad!* As frightened as she was, she never mentioned this episode to anybody—not to her mother and not to any of her siblings. The family's pattern of secrecy was too deeply ingrained in her.

The beatings went on, worse than ever before. A pall of despair settled over the family again. The difference between the peaceful months when their father was away at the mental hospital and the miserable present was so stark that it was unbearable.

In her hopelessness, Laura turned to books for an escape. She loved to read, so she visited the school library often. While reading a library book, she learned about tarot cards and how to predict the future with them. *Maybe I could use them to predict my future*, she thought.

Laura had no tarot cards and no money to buy any, but further reading revealed that ordinary playing cards could be used to divine the future in the same way. A deck of cards was easy to find in her house, and she experimented with them, trying to develop the skill of reading fortunes. She read several library books on how to read tarot cards or regular cards to predict the future, but she never became very skilled at it.

Joan and Cliff had left home by this time, leaving fewer kids to bear the brunt of their father's anger. Except for Bill, Laura and the other younger ones suffered more than ever before. In order to protect the farm's baby calves, Bill was assigned with trapping as many coyotes as possible to keep the coyote population on the ranch down to below two hundred. As a result, he was in the fields most of the time, unaware of what was happening in the house. He would get two dollars per coyote—good money for a kid—and he enjoyed the work.

Laura had twenty dental fillings about this time, and shortly afterward she began feeling sick. It wasn't anything specific. It felt like a general sense of ill health, and it became harder to handle the household's constant stress. Worst of all, she became depressed and persistently looked on the negative side of life. Despite the wretchedness of her home life, she was always able to count on her naturally resilient, optimistic attitude. Now it was gone.

Feeling as badly as she did, the whole situation of life with their dad appeared even bleaker than usual. Their mother wasn't going to leave. There was no way out, but something had to change. She couldn't take it anymore. She didn't know what was happening to her, but something was draining away her bodily reserves. At fourteen, she felt exhausted, worn out, and hopelessly depressed.

For weeks, she dragged herself through her chores, feeling miserable, both physically and emotionally; finally, one June day she decided that she had had enough. She wasn't going to get up at four the next morning. The cows would have to wake themselves. She would run away from home for a few days, and then she would make a grand entry and come back home. She imagined a big homecoming scene, and when she was welcomed back with outcries of joy by her mother and her siblings, she would insist once again that her mother do something to make things better.

She secretly packed some food in a paper grocery bag—a few jars of home-canned peaches and green beans and some sandwiches—and quietly left home. She walked a mile or two down the road until she came to a grassy ditch on a neighboring ranch. There she lay down and went to sleep. She slept for three days, waking up only to eat and drink some water from the natural spring by the woods.

After three days, she woke up feeling rested, stronger, and more optimistic about life. She had better go home. No doubt everyone missed her and worried about her. She timed her return for five o'clock, to coincide with her mother's return from work.

Laura walked into the house, wearing her cheeriest smile. "I'm here! I'm home!"

Mary Sicking was busy in the kitchen with her back to Laura when she walked into the house. Without even turning around, her mother said in an indifferent tone of voice, "That's nice. Where have you been?" Her tired and distracted mother hadn't even missed her! There were no search parties or questions about where she had been for three days. No one noticed but Bill. And he noticed only because he had to do her share of the chores as well as his own. As always, he kept to the code of silence, protecting Laura by taking on the extra work without saying a word. Laura was back with her family, and she had never felt so lonely and unloved in all her life. *I'm on my own!* she thought. *I have to take care of myself because I can't expect others to care about me.*

Laura's plan to improve her home situation by running away had accomplished exactly nothing. There was only one way left to fix things! Everyone recognized that the problem was their father. If he was gone permanently, life would return to the peaceful existence of the previous summer. The answer was simple: their dad needed to die.

"We have to kill Dad," Mark whispered one day after a terrible beating. He and Laura were sitting under the elm tree in the front yard, enjoying a brief break from farmwork.

Laura nodded. In any other family, Mark's words might have sounded preposterous but not in the Sicking family. These two had had about all they could take. Even though they knew it was evil, they were going to make it happen this time. "How are we gonna do it?" Laura asked.

"Let's just get one of the guns and shoot him."

"Which gun should we use?" Laura was straightforward. She wasn't afraid of guns, and she knew it wouldn't be hard to get their hands on one. There were several rifles and other firearms around the place, and none of them were locked up. Guns were a fact of life on the Texas ranch. All of the Sicking children knew how to handle a gun. They had used a .38-caliber revolver for target practice and shot beer cans off a fence.

"Let's use the .38," said Mark. "It's the easiest to hide." The two kids, one fourteen years old and the other thirteen, put their heads together and seriously schemed to murder their father.

Their older sister Lois, who was sixteen, happened to walk by. "What's going on?" she asked. Lois was overweight, although she was not nearly as obese as their dad. She was the number-one target of their father's verbal abuse. Despite his own size, he tormented Lois constantly about her weight, sneering in her face and calling her Fatso instead of using her name. The other children were called stupid and ugly, but Fatso was reserved for Lois.

Laura looked up at her sister. "We're making a plan to kill Dad." Lois sat down next to Laura and Mark. She hated their father just as much as they did. She knew they weren't kidding. She could tell by the looks on their faces that her two younger siblings were dead serious. They were all trying to survive.

"You guys, you can't do that! What you're talking about is called first-degree murder. You'll go to prison! You'll ruin your lives! You have to put that idea out of your heads right now. It's not worth it!" After a short while, Lois got up and walked away toward the house.

Mark looked at Laura with shock on his face. "Prison!" he said.

Laura replied, "We can't do this and go to prison, Mark!"

Mark sighed, and his shoulders drooped with hopelessness. "Yeah, you're right. We can't do it. We can't kill Dad."

Many years later, in a college psychology class, Laura would read a book on parricide. One line in the first chapter stood out: "Children between the ages of twelve and seventeen who kill their parents were more than just abused. They were tortured." She understood the truth of that sentence.

Was she a victim? Laura realized that she thought of herself that way. But being a victim wasn't safe. Things went from bad to worse for victims. For the first time in her life, it occurred to her that her own attitude might be part of what made her a victim. Somehow she needed to change it, but the strength to do so wasn't there, at least not yet. One more event would happen before this attitude change occurred—an event that would be the turning point in how Laura viewed herself.

CHAPTER 7

....

I Know, I'll Be a Doctor!

Laura took stock of her situation. Running away didn't work. No one except Bill even missed her. Her mom was too busy. Her siblings were too caught up in their own despair to be of any help. She couldn't depend on her family for anything. Killing her father would lead to a life in prison. And she was only fourteen, so there were four years before she could leave the house. She was on her own! She took several weeks to consider what options remained to her.

Slowly, she arrived at a single conclusion: suicide. No matter how bad things had gotten, she had never contemplated killing herself. But now she believed that all other possibilities were exhausted, and killing herself was her only way out. She knew suicide was bad, but she wasn't concerned about what was bad anymore. She would forget about religion.

The church had let her down too. The atmosphere and beauty of Sacred Heart Catholic Church, which had once brought her joy and solace, now just reminded her of her many sins and made her feel even more guilty. She knew that no amount of good deeds could save her. Besides, she couldn't afford to buy the candles.

Laura slowly began to see Catholicism as false and abusive in the same way her supposedly devout Catholic home was false and abusive. She lost faith in the priests. They told her mother she couldn't use birth control or get a divorce. In her opinion, that was stupid. The church was a sham—just a moneymaking machine.

Laura gave up on the Catholic Church. She no longer wanted to be a nun. She thought about her system of tracking her sins and her good deeds. Out of the seven years that she kept an account of her spiritual performance, there were only two days when she judged herself as good.

She was fourteen years old, and she realized that she couldn't do enough good deeds to offset the evilness that pushed her to despair about her spiritual condition. She gave up trying. But part of her still believed that God was loving and fair. *Maybe He will show me mercy and justice, in spite of what I have done*, she thought. *Maybe He will understand my situation enough so that I won't go to hell.*

Outwardly, she continued to go through the motions because she didn't want God to strike her dead. Laura still feared God. God and the Catholic Church were now completely separate in her mind.

But fear was the operative word. She was extremely scared of God, and she had no doubt that God was watching her to judge her. However, she was finished with praying to Him. She never doubted God's existence, but she was really, really mad at Him because He hadn't answered her prayers and changed her home life. She stopped talking to God for the next ten years.

It would be another five years before she would stop attending Mass and ten years before she would make the break with the church publicly.

For days, Laura continued to turn the idea of suicide over and over in her head. In the end, she made up her mind. She would do it. Once she had made her decision, then she spent days carefully planning each step. First, she thought about how to do it. Shooting herself in the head seemed the obvious choice. She was comfortable with guns, and she saw her father shoot animals that way. She knew where her father kept the always-loaded .38 revolver. She would have no problem getting the gun.

Next, she planned the time. She would do it during the week. She would pretend to be sick and stay home from school. Nobody would care enough to notice that she wasn't really ill. Her mom would be at her job in town, her dad would be out in the fields or in his shop, and the rest of the kids would be at school. She selected the date, a week away, in April.

Then she chose the place. She would do it in the tank room of the milking barn. The tank room was the only place where Laura was sure she could be alone. There was no privacy in the house—and there never was. The tank room was next to the milking parlor. It was a square white room, empty except for a giant steel milk-cooling tank.

Laura made her plans, visualizing each step in her mind, and carefully weighed the pros and cons, considering the method and the place. She never voiced these thoughts out loud and never shared her plan with another soul.

Her plan was complete. There was only one thing left to do: write the suicide note. From her school book bag, she took a new yellow pencil and a notebook and began to write.

She addressed it to her mother—the person she blamed for not protecting her. Her mother didn't miss Laura when she ran away, but she would be forced to notice when they found her body. She began to list her reasons for taking her life in plain, simple words: "Life is unbearable here. I can't take the violence. I can't handle watching the beatings anymore. It is just so crazy. I—"

Stop! Don't do it! They will be happy!

The thought was entirely in her mind, but the words were so emphatic that they surprised her. The message came again, loud and unbidden: *Stop! Don't do it! They will be happy!*

She stopped writing. She was shocked by this unwelcome thought. It wasn't her thought. Her mind was made up. Her suicide was a closed subject.

Yet, she found herself talking back to the thought in her head. "Who are 'they'? Who will be happy?" No answer came. None. Just the thought, stronger than ever: *Stop! Don't do it! They will be happy!*

"Look," Laura was clearly talking to herself now, "I cannot handle my home the way it is. I've already tried running away, and that didn't work. I can't kill Dad, so this is the only choice left!"

Pick something in life and succeed, the thought came.

"What?"

Prove them wrong! Become great!

Laura was stunned. Suddenly, everything was different. "That's a great idea! That's what I should do. I'll show them!" She balled up the suicide note, and the thoughts of killing herself left her mind. Her head was filled with the prospect of becoming successful and great.

She went for a long walk in the woods. Slowly, a plan began to take shape in her mind. She would start her life over. She would forget the old Laura—a helpless, weak, lonely, suffering, bad child that bad things happened to—a child nobody loved. She would put that part of her life behind her. Then she would become a new person—strong, smart, attractive, admired, and above all, successful. Her miserable childhood would be erased from her thoughts as though it had never been.

It was an imaginative way for a fourteen-year-old child to deal with an intolerable situation. The fact that it would be impossible to do it on her own wouldn't be clear to her for many years.

For the first time in her life, Laura felt hopeful. She allowed herself to contemplate a grand future, a future where she would be safe and happy for many years ahead.

Fortified by her newfound resolve, Laura found that the wretchedness at home took on less importance. She no longer looked to her family for any support, much less for love or kindness. A new, hard-edged optimism and self-reliance filled her, and her mind was awhirl with hope.

Everyone will be surprised and amazed when I become a success, she thought. From that day on, she decided to stop thinking like a victim. She would no longer expect love or support from anyone in the family. Expecting it and not getting it had made her feel like a victim of their rejection. She would give herself positive affirmations and not expect them from her family. *You have good qualities. Dwell on them. Stop putting yourself down*, she told herself. She also decided that she must accept her situation in life, face it with courage, and do everything she could to get herself out of it. No one was going to do it for her.

Suck it up! You're going to have to be tough if you're going to be successful. Don't worry if other people are tough on you. Be even tougher on yourself! No more emotions! Emotions are for sissies! Quit crying. Quit feeling sorry for yourself. There are people who have much harder lives than you do. From that point on, she never cried again. It would be ten years before her tears returned.

Always practical, Laura spent a lot of time thinking about what success meant. How would she know when she was successful? And more important, how would her family know? What would impress them the most?

After much serious thought, she narrowed it down to a short list of three things that would make her successful and happy. First, she needed to be rich. Second, she would have to be a sophisticated, cultured person. And third, she had to be beautiful. Rich, sophisticated, and beautiful—that's how she defined success. It was simple!

OK, she thought. *I have to go to college, like Mom said. But I can't get just an ordinary degree. I have to pick something that will earn a lot of money so that I can support myself with a good standard of living. I'll be a doctor! Doctors make the most money.* Money would make her happy.

Sophistication was next on her list. *I need to read more books*, she thought. *I need to read books on all of the topics that sophisticated people might discuss, such as science, art, music, history, and politics—stuff like that. I'll need books on etiquette and good manners, too, so I'll know how to mix with other wealthy people.*

Beauty was the third item in her plan. That was a hard one. For as long as she could remember, her father had told her she was ugly, ugly and stupid. She could see how a person could do something about being stupid by studying hard and reading lots of books, but beautiful? That was a difficult one until she thought of plastic surgery. That was it!

Now she had a plan. She would go to college, become a doctor, make a lot of money, learn how to be sophisticated, and have plastic surgery to become beautiful. Nothing was going to get in her way. *Nothing*. Not a husband—she had already made up her mind that she would never marry. Why marry if she knew she would be beaten? Not children. Why would she bring kids into the world to suffer the misery and violence she had known? None of that stuff. Family relationships were not safe. On the other hand, dating, she decided, was good—as long as she stayed away from farm boys. She enjoyed the company of boys as much as she enjoyed her younger brothers. If a boy ever made her feel unsafe, she would just leave.

She would go to California as soon as she could. She had never been there, but she knew from the Beach Boys' songs that California was where rich, sophisticated, beautiful people lived. Texas was the land of slavery and unhappiness. She would turn her back on the whole state and anything that had to do with farming and never again work as hard as she did at home.

Laura soon realized that she needed to start making changes right away. Up to this time, her grades were just OK—a mix of As and Bs with an occasional C. Another light went on in Laura's head. Grades were very important!

That very day Laura started doing her homework during every spare moment. She began reading constantly—carrying a book everywhere she went, even to the milking barn.

Laura also made a change in her diet as part of her plan to be the person she wanted to be. She saw several things on the farm that persuaded her to avoid eating pork and meat that had blood veins and bones. These events and others like them inclined Laura toward becoming a vegetarian.

In a few weeks, Laura went from hopeless and suicidal to driven—her focus zeroed in on success as she saw it. Her family hardly noticed the changes; but inside, she was becoming a different person. For the next ten years, Laura clung to this strategy for her future.

Success became the wall that protected her from her agony and that shielded her from loneliness, from her father's anger, and from the lack of her mother's love. She used all of her strength to reject negatives about herself. She would do her best to forget that the weak, helpless child she was even existed. But while Laura didn't like that child—hated her even—the fact still remained that little girl was a part of who she was.

CHAPTER 8

....

"You Have No Idea How Lucky You Are, Young Lady!"

Laura enrolled at Muenster High School with her mind focused on her strategy for success. She planned to have fun, but without realizing what she was doing, she took steps to freeze her emotions. She would invest her energy in relationships but only to a point. Other people couldn't really know her.

She got involved with the track team. She turned out to be the fastest long-distance female runner in the school, winning meet after meet, and her popularity grew. She wanted very much to be popular and to make friends, and she did. But she could not let her friends know the suffering child who lived deep inside her—the emotionally needy little girl who feared rejection and pain. This child was hidden from the world.

In grade school, she had wanted everybody to be her friend, but she was through with that. She adopted a new approach toward making friends. She needed friends who were safe and compassionate. Those would be her basic requirements for her friends.

In some ways, this newfound resolve was a good thing. Janelle was Laura's best friend through grade school, and she and Laura happily renewed their acquaintance in high school. But Janelle met and fell in love with a boy who was into drugs, and the two of them began to use marijuana. Janelle urged Laura to try a joint. "There is no way I'm going to do drugs with you! Drugs fry your brain. I'm going to college. I'm going to need my brain." The truth was she no longer felt safe with Janelle and dropped her old friend.

Laura became friends with Melissa, a fast runner on the girl's track team. Melissa's dad owned the bank in Muenster. They lived in a beautiful house by the lake. Melissa had all of the qualifications Laura wanted in a friend. Melissa's parents loved Laura, and she loved them. Their daughter was a bit wild and crazy, but they knew that Laura wasn't. Laura had high standards for herself—partly because of her long-term plan and partly because her mother always preached high moral standards to her children. She was still desperately trying to win her mother's love. She would do nothing that would go against her mother's wishes, at least, not yet.

Her high standards, good grades, and respectful manners impressed Melissa's parents. They insisted that Laura go everywhere with their daughter. In fact, they wouldn't let Melissa out of the house without Laura. They even took Laura with them on wonderful hiking and biking vacations to national parks.

Gina's parents also liked Laura. The three girls ran around together through high school. They went to football games together, and afterward, they gathered at the home of one or another of their friends.

As Laura entered her sophomore year of high school, things began changing at home. The older girls were moving out, and the remaining kids were growing up. It was getting easier for them to outrun their father. The beatings became less frequent.

Laura decided that as part of her new strategy for her life, she would no longer serve her father in the demeaning way he had always demanded. Never again would she wash his feet, clip his toenails and fingernails, fill his pipe, or lay out his clothes. She wasn't going to be his slave anymore! She just said no and ran outside. From then on, their dad had Bill do those tasks for him.

Although her dad was hitting the kids less frequently than he used to, he still was regularly beating her mom. But something else was changing too. The three younger brothers, Mark, Bryan, and Bill, were getting taller. Their dad was only five feet nine inches tall. His sons would grow to be more than six feet tall. Already their shoulders were wide, and they were muscular and strong as a result of hard labor on the farm. Their dad was still hugely overweight, and he was getting older. Physically, he was outmatched by his sons.

Mark came in from the barn one day and heard sounds of distress coming from the living room. He quickly strode into the room. His father had his mother cornered and was repeatedly hitting her with his fist. She was crying, screaming, and trying to ward off his blows, as she always did.

Mark didn't hesitate one second. With anger flashing in his eyes, he grabbed his father by the shirt front, slammed him against the wall, and held him there. "If I ever catch you beating Mom again, I will kill you," he shouted just inches from his father's face, with his voice loud and menacing.

Mark let go and his dad slumped against the wall, surprised at Mark's strength and uncharacteristic force. Then his dad turned on his heel and left the room without another word. He knew Mark meant every word he said. Mark was not the first of his children to threaten to kill him. Emmett Sicking never beat his wife in front of his children again, but they knew he continued to hit her when the kids weren't around.

Only a short time after this incident, their mother revealed to Bryan that their father had waited until everyone was out of the house, and when the coast was clear, he hit her again. This time it was Bryan's turn to threaten him. "I heard that you beat Mom again yesterday. If you do that one more time, I will find out. And I will kill you, Dad. Don't ever let me hear that you beat her again." Their father finally got the message. The fight had gone out of him. Emmett knew his children were growing up and that he couldn't treat them or their mother as he had in the past. The beatings and the verbal abuse completely stopped.

Mark was sixteen, and he wanted to go to college like his older sisters. He knew he needed money to buy a car, so, despite his dad's protests that he must work on the farm, he got a job at a cheese-making factory in Muenster. He worked a man's full shift every day after school. He worked for ten days in a row and was sleeping soundly one morning after getting off work at midnight the night before.

It was harvesttime, and Emmett needed Mark's help in the fields. "Come on, Mark, rise and shine!" His father was at the door of the boys' bedroom, shouting. "I need you out there stacking hay today."

"Dad," Mark replied sleepily, burrowing deeper under the covers, "I've worked ten long shifts in a row, and I'm exhausted! Please leave me alone. I need to sleep!"

Emmett's temper flared up. "You'll get up and get to work, Mark, or I'm kicking you out of this house," he yelled.

"OK, if that's what you want," Mark answered, more awake now. "I'll leave!" And he did, finding himself a room to rent in town while he continued to work at the cheese plant and go to school.

Laura admired her brother's ambition and persistence, but she felt sorry that it was Mark who was treated so unfairly and tossed out of the house at the young age of sixteen.

High school continued for Laura. She studied hard and made all As, winning the respect of her teachers. Her track career blossomed, and she enjoyed the resulting popularity. There was a group of six very smart boys in her class that the other kids called The Brains. The boys noticed that Laura was also doing well scholastically and welcomed her into their elite company, treating her like a sister. These boys met all of Laura's qualifications for friendship, but she never dated any of them. Rather, she enjoyed their companionship, much like she relished the company of her younger brothers when they were small.

Laura was sixteen when she went to the dentist again. The nearly twenty mercury amalgam fillings she got three years before were cracking and breaking down, causing her pain. The dentist removed and replaced them all. Not long afterward, she noticed that she was feeling unusually tired and dragged herself through her chores and her schoolwork, barely able to function.

Of course, she told no one how she was feeling. Then she began to notice that urinating was painful. Yet, she didn't tell anyone. The pain got worse each day, and one day she noticed that her urine was pink with blood. She was worried, but she still didn't mention it to anyone. As always, one didn't talk about that stuff in her family.

The next day her urine was red—all day. By the following day, it turned black. Now there was no pain at all, only numbness, and she was convinced that she was going to die. Her fear finally forced her to tell her mother, who immediately drove her to the Muenster Memorial Hospital, where she worked. The emergency room doctor took one look at Laura and admitted her immediately. She was experiencing kidney failure.

The next thing Laura knew she was lying on a narrow, white gurney, squinting up at bright overhead lights. In preparation for an X-ray of her kidneys, a contrast dye was injected into her arm. Almost immediately, her body went into convulsions, oscillating on the table like a flopping fish. She heard doctors and nurses shouting in panic, and then everything went black.

Laura passed out.

She spent a week in the hospital, sleeping almost around the clock, waking only to eat a little. The doctors concluded that her kidneys were attacked by a staph infection, and they gave her massive amounts of antibiotics to combat it.

The day she was to be released from the hospital, she was taken to Dr. Kralick's office. She was very weak and unable to stand for more than a few minutes. She sank gratefully into a chair. Dr. Kralick walked in. He was getting older, and his hair was turning gray. His manner on this day was very stern, so serious that he frightened an already petrified Laura even more. He looked her straight in the eye and launched into the strongest sermon she had ever heard in her life.

"You have no idea how lucky you are, young lady!" he began. "You came very close to dying in the emergency room. When your kidneys didn't respond to the treatment and hadn't started working by the third day after you were admitted, we almost put you on dialysis. If that had happened, you might have lived the rest of your life dependent on a dialysis machine—and most patients on dialysis live five years or less. But we decided to wait one more day. And, on the morning of the fourth day, your kidneys started working again.

"So from now on," he continued, "you are going to have to make some serious changes. You must take care of your body—especially your kidneys—if you want to live." Then Dr. Kralick leaned even closer to Laura, and his eyes never left her face. "Hear me and hear me well, young lady. You cannot drink alcohol ever again. You cannot drink coffee, tea, Coke, or anything else with caffeine. These things stress your kidneys, and you cannot afford to do that."

"OK," Laura whispered. "I understand. Thank you for telling me, Doctor Kralick." Frightened right down to the soles of her feet, Laura tried hard to do what he said when she returned to her life. She tried hard to stop drinking alcohol. The problem was, though, that she found it difficult to go to a teenage drinking party with her friends and not drink beer. She learned to make half a glass of beer last through an entire party by taking only an occasional sip. But she didn't quit drinking altogether.

One good thing came out of Laura's illness. Dr. Kralick had a talk with her parents. "Your daughter can no longer do hard manual labor," he warned them. "Her body is physically unable to take that kind of work." Laura never milked another cow or stacked another hay bale, and she got to sleep in until six o'clock every morning.

Her badly compromised body suffered in other ways. For years, she was plagued with severe, itchy rashes all over her body. Only cortisone shots brought her any relief until a college chemistry professor happened to remark that her rash might be linked to a calcium deficiency. She bought some drugstore calcium pills, and after only a week, her rash disappeared, never to return.

Slowly, Laura's kidneys restored themselves, and her health improved; but it was seven long months before she was strong enough to participate in another track meet.

On the outside, Laura was making a success of high school despite her health problems. Inside, however, she remained closed off—her emotions frozen— driven entirely by her steely resolve to obtain success as she defined it for herself. Maintaining a cheerful, fun-loving exterior while not feeling deep emotions was hard work. Although she rejected the authoritative, conservative German Catholic view of God and turned her back on the church, she was drawn to the presence of God in nature—a source of comfort and solace that never let her down and that never asked anything in return.

One summer day their dad assigned Laura to watch the cattle in a field that had no fences, forcing her to stay out there the whole day. It was a very hot August afternoon, and she was sitting under a tree, trying to stay cool, and idly watching the cattle grazing in the softly waving golden prairie grass in the field just across the road.

Suddenly, she saw a bolt of dry lightning strike the field. The tinder-dry grass immediately burst into flames. The cows ran one way, and the flames went the other. The flames appeared to swirl and dance as a sudden wind blew them across the field, creating a roaring wall of fire that devoured everything in its path. Then the flames reached the road and the green field beyond, and the fire died out as quickly as it started, leaving total devastation behind.

Laura sat transfixed, staring at the naked, black, still-smoking field. In only a few seconds, everything changed. The power of that lightning bolt and the fire that followed it was staggering. The field looked destroyed.

Later, she told her father about what she saw, thinking he would be upset about the loss of the pasture. But her father wasn't concerned. "Yeah, that's the way nature works," he said. "The ashes provide nutrients that the soil needs. You watch; next year the grass will grow back even stronger and taller." Skeptical, Laura kept an eye on that field the following year to see if her father was right; sure enough, what he said was true. *So that is how nature works*, she marveled. *New life and strength follow destruction.*

A thought came to her mind. *Is it possible that the bad things in my life, the things that nearly destroyed me, could somehow transform me into a genuinely stronger, better person?* It was only a thought—but a beautiful thought. For just a moment, she felt a tiny glimmer of hope—a sense that the blackness inside her might someday be replaced by something much better.

CHAPTER 9

....

Come On, Mom! Fight for Us!

L aura did so well on the track team in high school that she was offered a full athletic scholarship to Texas Woman's University in Denton, Texas. Her parents didn't want her to take it. They didn't believe that women should be seen running in public and found it embarrassing. Her parents also said they were worried she would spend too much time running and not enough time studying. Laura wasn't sure that she could maintain her grades while running; so, under pressure from her parents, she turned down the scholarship.

Cliff and Joan, Laura's older siblings, had both left home by this time. With his childhood injuries far behind him, Cliff became Muenster High School's star football athlete. He was so good, in fact, that he earned a full college athletic scholarship. Unfortunately, he was badly injured in a game, so he left college, came home to Muenster, got a job working with the local telephone company, and married Kathy, his high-school sweetheart.

Joan, always extremely smart and capable, was the valedictorian of her senior class at Sacred Heart High School. After graduation, she stayed home for a couple of years and worked at the local sewing factory before getting married to James, who was a brilliant young man from a local German Catholic family. Both saved their money and put each other through college and earned advanced degrees.

Fortunately for Laura, she had another older sister who paved the way for her younger siblings to go to college. Joyce was ready for college about the time that Laura started high school. Laura knew, even then, that Joyce had big dreams for herself. She remembered seeing something that Joyce had written on the wall of the barn. Laura was walking by the fence that surrounded the corral where the cattle were penned before milking. She noticed something carefully written with a pencil high up on the side of the barn on the rough metal siding.

Curious, she climbed up onto the fence to see what it said: "I dream about my future. I want to go to college and become a nurse. I might even go to medical school. I want to move to California and have a happy life. I want out of here!" It was signed "Joyce."

The family rule, up to that time, was that the Sicking children were not allowed to work for anyone but their father while they were in high school. Their parents couldn't provide money for college, and without a part-time job during high school, the kids were unable to save any money to help themselves. College, at least right after high school, wasn't financially an option.

So Joyce graduated from high school with excellent grades and no money. She was very intelligent and extremely driven to succeed. She was strong, feisty, and determined to get a college education—no matter what. Her mother supported her. Her father didn't. Mary Sicking stuck to her guns. She wanted her daughters to be independent, so they could leave a bad marriage someday if they had to. But in Emmett Sicking's mind, his daughters had two choices: stay at home and work on the farm all their lives, or get married. He didn't see higher education for girls as important.

One night after dinner, Laura, who was only fourteen at the time, happened to be in the living room while her parents were arguing about Joyce's desire to go to college. Laura's ears pricked up, and she listened carefully, thinking, *Come on, Mom! Fight for us! Give Joyce a chance!* She wasn't especially close to her sister, but she wanted to go to college, too, and she could see that her life was also tied up in this argument.

"There's no point in discussing this again," Emmett said.

"But she needs to go!"

"Mary, you know we don't have the money to send her to college!" In Emmett's mind, that was the end of the matter. But Mary Sicking wasn't to be put off that easily. She continued the argument, and finally, she wrung a concession from her husband. Joyce could go to college, but she would go with no money—nothing, not for tuition, not for room and board, not for books—nothing. It was an impossible arrangement, but as Laura would later learn, maybe not as crazy as it sounded.

Joyce was a pretty girl—slim, with curly blond hair. The girls were allowed to babysit in their spare time after chores, and Joyce managed to save up a little money for clothes. She packed the clothes into two small suitcases, and her mother drove her to Grayson County College, near Denison, Texas, a town about an hour's drive away from Muenster.

"Good luck, Joyce. I'll come back and get you at Thanksgiving." Mary waved and drove away, leaving her daughter standing in front of the low red-brick buildings of the community college.

In this situation, Joyce was resourceful. As the oldest daughter living at home, she was entrusted by her mother with the responsibility of paying the household bills. When she left home, she took the family checkbook with her. Joyce wrote checks for one semester's tuition, dormitory fees, and books. She wrote another check for a used car and quickly found herself a waitressing job in the nearby town of Sherman, Texas. Although she was as frugal as possible, she ran up an overdraft of more than five thousand dollars.

Back in Muenster, her father got an urgent call from the bank. The checks were bouncing. Emmett was furious. After he calmed down, he and Mary were forced to go into town and take out a bank loan to cover the shortfall. "This is what happens when the kids aren't allowed to get jobs while they're still in high school," Mary told her husband, driving her point home relentlessly. "The kids must have a car. The only way they'll ever get one is to get a part-time job while they're still in high school and save their money."

While she had no doubt that what Joyce did was wrong, Laura admired her sister's resourcefulness. She never found out whether her mom knew in advance about Joyce's plan to use the checkbook, but Joyce did well for herself. By working hard and being careful with her money, she was able to earn enough to pay her own way after that first semester. Her dad finally got the point. From then on, the kids were allowed to get part-time jobs during their last two years in high school.

Most of the girls got jobs as waitresses at Rohmer's Restaurant in Muenster. It was an old-fashioned, family-owned German restaurant. Laura started there as soon as she recovered from her kidney failure, grateful for the chance to earn money for a car.

It took her two years of waitressing to save up enough money; but by her eighteenth birthday, Laura had saved enough to buy a car for college. Laura appreciated her dad's expertise as a mechanic and realized she needed his help to buy the right car. He was happy to help. After Mark's and Bryan's confrontations with their dad a couple of years before, Emmett's behavior changed so that he no longer frightened Laura physically and she was comfortable being with him. Her father spent a day driving her around in the pickup to used-car lots, looking for the best car her twelve hundred dollars would buy. Together they selected a brown 1972 Chevy Vega. It wasn't the most beautiful car in the world, but it looked great to her.

Laura enrolled at Grayson County College in 1976. She was on her way! She was still planning to be a doctor, or maybe a pharmacist. Her premed classes included chemistry, math, and physics. She found her classes to be interesting and was soon doing well academically. In a few weeks, she found a part-time waitressing job nearby, and she attended Mass every Sunday.

Adjusting to dormitory life took a little longer. She slipped into some bad habits. The freedom to go out to clubs, to dance and to drink whenever she wanted, tempted her, despite her resolve to get good grades and succeed at college. One Saturday night she went out to a club and drank, partied, and danced until five o'clock in the morning. She came home and slept until two o'clock on Sunday afternoon.

She woke up, looked blearily at the clock on her bedside table, and sat up, suddenly terror stricken. Two o'clock in the afternoon! She had missed the last Mass! She was afraid of God's retribution for missing Mass. She remembered what Sister Aloysia said about the vengeful, wrathful, authoritative God who would certainly strike her dead. She stayed in her room all the rest of that day, doing her homework, too afraid to leave. When nothing happened that day, she stayed in her room all of the following week, except for walking to classes. Maybe God was being merciful to her because she hadn't intentionally overslept. She thought about it and puzzled over it for the entire week. Why didn't God punish her?

So, as a test, the next Sunday she skipped Mass on purpose. Nothing happened. She skipped Mass for the next four months and still no lightning and no car wreck.

Laura's last bit of belief in the German Catholic Church that she grew up in was shattered by this experience. She had lost faith in the rituals of the church before this, but she still believed what she was told about the character and wrath of God. Now, all the things she was taught by the nuns, by the priests, and by her mother weren't true. Sister Aloysia had lied. She *lied*!

Laura's distrust of the Catholic Church and her disillusionment with its doctrines were solidified further because of this experience, until she actually began to hate the church of her childhood. She was filled with confusion. Had she lost all chance of getting into heaven because of the Catholic Church's false teachings? Being lied to about the very nature of God's character seemed like a serious violation of her trust. Indeed, Laura felt deeply violated. Her whole faith was based on what she was told. Now everything was gone.

During the next several years, Laura slowly came to understand that the teachings of the conservative European Catholic Church set her mother up for suffering. Mary Sicking believed that she had no choice but to stay married to Emmett and allow the abuse of herself and her children to continue.

Emmett was a nominal Catholic. Like all his German Catholic neighbors, he was raised in the Catholic Church; but for him, religion didn't guide his life. Despite his problems, he was an extremely intelligent, inquisitive, and analytical man. He wasn't a particularly religious man though. It was Mary's unwavering faith in this traditional European Catholic doctrine that forced her and her children to remain trapped in the prison created by Emmett's anger and violence.

Mary believed that divorce was wrong under any circumstances, that birth control was never to be condoned, and that her salvation depended on her raising a large Catholic family. She believed that she must say the same rote prayers, that she must never question the priests or the church, and that she must not read the Bible for herself. She lived her life by these traditions and doctrines, and the result was the abusive home life that Laura and her siblings endured for years.

Now Laura saw these doctrines as evil and dangerous. She realized that the beliefs a person has describe the God he or she serves. A God that condemns divorce for all reasons, she reasoned, must also be a God who says a woman must stay married even if she is beaten and her children are molested.

A God who condemns all birth control must also be a God who says a woman should get pregnant even if it kills her. This God supported the oppression of women. The traditional European Catholic doctrine her mother lived by supported the subjugation of women. The God they described oppressed people. Laura fully rejected such a view of God and truth.

Laura reached these conclusions alone. As always, she didn't share her feelings or her thoughts with anyone else. She arrived at her view of the Catholic Church independently, and for a long time, she believed she was the only one who believed this way.

What other lies did they teach me? Laura wondered. *I have no idea what's true and what's not. Do I believe God exists?* She thought back to her earliest childhood memories—to the time when she felt that God was her best Friend. She couldn't deny the peace and happiness that experience gave her then. *Yes, God exists*, she decided. *But I don't know anything about Him.* Where could she turn for answers?

For years, she had been told how evil Protestants were. She didn't know what a Protestant actually was, but she knew they weren't Catholic. That seemed like a good place to start. She decided to systematically attend every non-Catholic church listed in the Sherman-Denison Yellow Pages, starting with A. She would get literature on what a denomination believed and how it was founded. Then she would visit its church service.

She told her roommate, Julie, about her plan. "I'll take you to my church," Julie offered. The next Sunday she accompanied Julie to the Church of Christ. The church was plain and unadorned inside. This was far different from the marble, candles, statues, and incense of Catholic worship that she was used to, but Laura didn't even mind. It was the pastor's preaching that demanded her attention because it was full of fire and brimstone. "You sinners are going to hell unless you repent!" he screamed.

The yelling and shouting continued for two and a half hours, and the man showed no sign of slowing down. Laura had heard plenty of verbal abuse in her young life, and she didn't like it. The words were different, but this sounded too much like one of her father's rants. "Julie, I can't take any more. I have to leave," she pleaded. So the girls left, and Laura crossed the Church of Christ off her list. She never knew whether that pastor was typical of the denomination or not.

Laura spent the next three years investigating all of the churches in the Yellow Pages before she left Christianity altogether and started to study other world religions.

It was while she was attending Grayson County College that Laura and Joyce became closer. Laura admired Joyce and appreciated that she paved the way for her to go to college. Joyce earned her nursing degree at Grayson and became a nurse anesthetist, earning a master's degree in that field. While working at a Houston hospital, she began another master's degree in biophysics in preparation for medical school.

Joyce worked hard and overcame many odds to get where she was, and Laura admired her tenacity. Joyce was smart, tough, and accomplished—everything Laura wanted to be. Physically, she and Joyce were a lot alike; both were petite, blond, and pretty. Both had apparently happy-go-lucky, outgoing personalities. Laura also admired Joyce's ease in social situations. She was popular with the opposite sex and dated lots of men.

Joyce became Laura's role model. Extremely intelligent and inquisitive, she was as well read as Laura. She sent Laura many books on a wide variety of subjects, from Catholicism to yoga, and Laura read them all. The ones she enjoyed, she would add to her growing library; the ones she didn't, she would trade in at a local used bookstore for more books.

Laura continued to do well in her college classes. She missed one thing, however, and that thing was running. Always a high-energy person, Laura found sitting through class for four or five hours to be torture, no matter how much she enjoyed the lectures. Milking cows for three and a half hours before going to school as a kid used up enough energy so that she could sit through her classes.

So she started running every morning. She ran through the quiet country campus and along the flat surrounding roads for a couple of miles, enjoying nature and the cool early morning air. That took the edge off her energy, and she was able to sit through her classes without a problem.

Soon she ran five or more seven-minute miles every morning. Running was addictive and euphoric. She would get lost in it. It did more than control her excess energy; it took her sadness and anger away, and made her happy for several hours.

Without ever joining the track team or attracting a coach's attention, she was soon signing up for half marathons that were fund-raisers for various causes, such as fighting muscular dystrophy or heart disease. Her outgoing personality made it easy for her to get people to donate money. She even won a bicycle that way, and a highly complimentary article about her running and fund-raising appeared in the Lubbock, Texas, newspaper.

At nineteen years old, a few months into her sophomore year, Laura found herself back in her hometown dentist's office, in pain from cracked and broken fillings. For the third time, her old mercury amalgam fillings were removed and replaced with new ones. Afterward, she felt weak and tired, with no energy, and was plagued with a low-grade fever and a runny nose. She couldn't run. She struggled to keep up with her classes and get her homework done.

She went home to see Dr. Kralick every Friday for almost two months. He gave her several different antibiotics, but none of them worked. He had no other answers outside of admonishing her to get more rest. One Friday Dr. Kralick was called away, and Laura saw his partner, who was a young Cuban immigrant. She told this young doctor how she was feeling.

"I would like to run a blood test," he responded. Laura waited while they processed the sample. He walked into the examination room with the results of the blood tests in his hand.

"What have you been eating?" he asked. "Tell me what you eat in a typical day."

Laura was surprised by this question and replied, "For breakfast, I usually have two or three cups of coffee and two or three doughnuts. For lunch, I have some potato chips, a Diet Coke, and a hot fudge sundae with my roommate. Then for dinner, we have a banana split."

"Get off the junk food!" the doctor practically roared. "You don't have any nutrition in your body! What did you grow up eating?"

"Well, I grew up on a farm, so we had lots of meat, potatoes, bread, cheese, vegetables, and fruit."

"Go back to that," he replied. The doctor continued, "Your tests show that your blood is very low in minerals. You need to take a mega-multi-mineral supplement that you can get at a health-food store."

This advice made a lot of sense to Laura. She remembered mineral blocks on the farm. Her parents bought both mineral blocks and salt blocks for the cattle. The pastures were dotted with the white salt blocks and the red mineral blocks that contained calcium, magnesium, phosphorus, and other minerals the cows needed to remain healthy. The cows could be seen regularly licking the blocks.

She remembered one spring when expenses were high and money was especially tight on the farm that her parents decided to buy only salt blocks and forgo the more expensive mineral blocks. Things went well for several months, but then the cattle began to fall ill. Several animals were unable to get off the ground, and others could hardly walk. The entire herd looked sick and weak.

With their livelihood threatened, her panicked parents called the veterinarian. He took one look at the herd and asked, "Are you giving them minerals? Where are their mineral blocks?"

"We stopped buying them," Emmett said. "They just got too expensive."

The vet shook his head in exasperation. "That's why your cows are sick. That's why they can't walk! They have to have minerals! You need to get mineral blocks back in those pastures right away."

The Sickings bought the blocks immediately and placed them in the pastures. At first, Laura and the other kids had to physically help the cattle get to their feet and walk to the blocks. Once the cows began to lick the blocks, they quickly gained strength; in a few days, the herd was well and strong again.

Obviously, cattle need to have minerals, or they get sick and die. Evidently, the same is true for humans. Laura began taking the multimineral supplements, just as the doctor ordered, and her health improved dramatically. Finally, she began to get the point. Getting enough of the right minerals in one's diet was necessary for good health. Everything a person puts in his or her mouth is important. While she saw what eating sugar did to her father, she thought that was just his problem up until then. She realized then that she needed to learn how to eat a healthier diet as part of her plan for success.

She dug into all of the books about food and diet she could find. She didn't waste her time on fiction. She always enjoyed reading, but now she was reading for guidance on how to live a healthy life.

She read several books that enumerated the evils of smoking. Her father smoked, and Laura always hated it. It made her lungs ache and her eyes burn. Now that she knew what a terrible poison it was, she vowed to avoid it.

Caffeine and alcohol were different, though. What she read about caffeine convinced her that she should stop drinking coffee, but it was a habit she couldn't kick. She knew that alcohol was a poison, and her reading only brought home its dangers more forcefully. But this knowledge and her willpower alone were not sufficient to rid her of her need to drink. It would take something greater than herself to empower her to make those changes—something or someone for whom she was still searching.

If any human being could have fixed herself by acquiring information or by sheer resolve and the power of her own will, Laura would have done it. In her determination to be successful, she was driven by a tremendous need to free herself of her past and obtain the happy, healthy, triumphant life she so desperately craved. But she was coming to the conclusion that she could not do this on her own. She needed help. But where would that help come from?

CHAPTER 10

....

"Did Anybody Ever Tell You How Beautiful You Are, Laura?"

Laura's health continued to improve with the multimineral supplements and her new diet, but her life stayed extremely busy. Between maintaining straight As in her eighteen credit hours of classes, working long hours at her part-time waitressing job, delving into all of the books on health and religion in the library, and sleeping, there wasn't enough time in the day. And there was never enough money. Her old Vega was wearing out. Fortunately, her father kept it repaired for her, but it was constantly in need of something.

She enjoyed running, reading, and her classes, but she didn't have time or money to have the type of fun that college students usually have. She had little time to date and no time to develop a relationship if she did. She went out with a fellow student named Ron a couple of times. Ron seemed like a nice boy until, on their second date, he asked her to marry him, causing Laura to freak out and drop him like a hot potato.

As her sophomore year continued, Laura was forced by her financial situation to reevaluate her long-term goals. She saw her future as a straight line and assumed that she would go right through college and on to medical school, but she hadn't realized how difficult working her way through was going to be. *I can't keep this pace up*, she thought despondently, frightened that she would fail at college.

Something had to change. Laura thought it through carefully. *I had better start thinking of my plan in terms of steps. A bachelor's degree is step one. A medical degree will be step two. I need to get a bachelor's degree in a field that will help fund my medical degree. Waitressing isn't going to do it.*

She was taking a calculus class that semester. Calculus was so much fun! She excelled at it so much that she took more calculus classes as electives. "You shouldn't go into medicine, Laura," her calculus instructor advised. "With your talent for math, you should go into engineering."

Laura pondered that advice. Should she change her life's goal? She valued Joan's judgment and asked her for an opinion. Joan, a chemist, was working as a lab analyst in Dallas. "Oh, yes, Laura," Joan agreed. "Get out of medicine and drug pushing! Go into chemical engineering."

So Laura took out a college loan, quit her waitressing job, and switched her major to chemical engineering. The chemistry classes would still prepare her for medical school or even pharmaceutical school, if she chose one of those careers, and engineering would lead to a well-paying job after college. She could graduate from college, work a few years to pay off her debts, and get herself a good car before starting medical school. College loans were scary, but failing at college because she couldn't pay her bills was even scarier.

Laura's mother strongly opposed her switching her major to chemical engineering. She was positive nobody would hire a female engineer, and Laura expected her to protest. Most of her daughters chose careers Mary Sicking considered appropriately female. Laura, on the other hand, had no qualms about choosing a male-dominated career field. She knew where her strengths lay, and anyway, it was in her nature to be a trailblazer.

Laura was enjoying the switch of her major to chemical engineering. One of her classes that semester was physics. She liked physics and was very good at it. She was making all As in the class. Her professor's name was Dick Ice. Dr. Ice was a tall, dignified-looking, gray-haired man of about sixty years old. Laura respected and admired him and was her usual friendly and outgoing self in his classes and labs.

One afternoon in the physics lab, Laura was working on an experiment with her lab partner, a hardworking young man. Most of the rest of the class had already finished their experiments for the day and had left the room. Laura and her partner and one other pair of students were still in the lab. Dr. Ice dismissed the other couple. Then he told Laura's partner he could go. Laura, the last student left in the room, hurried to get her things together to leave too.

When the young man left the room, Dr. Ice closed the door and stood for a moment with his back against it. Then he spoke Laura's name. She glanced up and saw Dr. Ice smile a lecherous smile.

"Did anybody ever tell you how beautiful you are, Laura?" he asked with a soft and insinuating voice. "You have a really gorgeous little figure," he continued. His eyes swept over her body while he began moving toward her—his intentions were all too clear.

A million panicky thoughts chased each other through Laura's mind in the course of a few seconds. This man held her future in his hands. A poor grade from him could keep her out of medical school. She knew exactly what he wanted. What should she do?

Well, I may never be a doctor, she decided while her rising anger gave her courage. *But I won't let this creep lay a hand on me. My safety is more important than my career.* She began backing up, feeling more frightened and alone as Dr. Ice kept coming toward her. *He's a lot bigger than I am,* she thought. *But I won't let him touch me, and I won't let him ruin everything I've worked and planned for.* He backed her into a small storage room and trapped her there.

Dr. Ice's right hand darted toward her body and fondled her breasts through her shirt. Then he moved his hand lower and unzipped her jeans. At the touch of his hand on her bare skin, sheer panic set in, and a sudden shot of adrenaline raced through Laura. She found the strength to shove him out of the way. She zipped up her pants and ran out of the room.

Shaking from head to foot, she found her way back to her dorm room. What should she do now? She knew she hadn't done anything to encourage this man, who was old enough to be her grandfather. She knew she needed to tell someone. Someone in authority needed to know what he had done, and she needed help to protect herself and other women from him. What Dr. Ice did filled her with an overwhelming sense of outrage and anger.

She talked to her chemistry professor. He was her mentor, and she trusted him more than anyone else on campus. He listened to her story quietly. When she finished, she asked, "Do you think I should go to the president's office and tell someone there?"

Her chemistry teacher nodded. "You're not the first student he's molested," he said quietly. "Dr. Ice has a reputation for that kind of behavior. As for talking to the president, yes, that is the process you should follow. But I would suggest that you go see the president's secretary first. Tell her what you have told me. She'll advise you what to do."

Laura went to see the president's secretary that afternoon. She was a middle-aged, motherly woman and a sympathetic listener. She listened attentively to Laura's story, then Laura asked, "What do you think I should do next? How do I handle telling the president?"

The older woman shook her head regretfully. "Laura, I have to be honest with you. Telling the president wouldn't do a bit of good. It could actually make things worse for you. Dr. Ice is a very good friend of our president. In fact, I know that both of them belong to a so-called sex club that holds parties off campus."

Laura's heart sank. "But what am I supposed to do?" she asked.

"The only thing you can do. Go back to class. Dr. Ice teaches the only physics course on campus, and you have to have that course. Just be sure you never allow yourself to be in a position where you are alone with that man again."

So Laura, feeling even more determined to protect herself, went back to the physics class. She told her two lab partners, both men, what happened. She asked them to protect her from Dr. Ice, and they agreed they would. She talked to the other two women in the class. Neither of them would acknowledge that anything similar had happened to them. They didn't want to talk about it, but Laura got the distinct impression that they, too, had to deal with Dr. Ice's inappropriate behavior.

The professor appeared to ignore her, and she kept her distance from him. Then it was time for another physics test. Laura knew she made an A. When Dr. Ice handed out the papers, he stopped at Laura's desk. "Well, Laura, you didn't do well on this test," he said. "Come by my office after class, and we can talk about what you can do to improve your grade."

"What grade did I make?"

"You got a B."

"I'll take the B," Laura replied. She knew she deserved an A, but she had no intention of going to his office. The next test was the final for that semester. Laura knew she did extremely well on it; in fact, she made certain that she earned an A. Again, as he passed out the papers, Dr. Ice stopped by Laura's desk.

"You didn't do very well at all on your final, Laura," he said, shaking his head. "Please come by my office this afternoon so that we can discuss it."

"What did I make on the test?"

"You got a C."

"And what does that give me for my final grade for the semester?"

"Your final grade is a B."

"I'll take the B."

Laura was extremely angry at this blatantly unfair treatment. She knew she deserved an A. Straight As were very important if she was to get into medical school, but it was more than that. Her rage was rooted in the helplessness she felt. This man had victimized her! She wasn't able to prevent this incident from happening or stop it from happening to others. She wasn't able to protect herself from the unfair treatment that followed. Nobody would help her. And she had to survive another whole semester with this professor!

All of the feelings of helplessness she had endured as a child flooded back. Once again she was the vulnerable, helpless little girl that bad things happened to. Was the incident with Dr. Ice another of those bad things? Despite all her efforts to put her childhood behind her, was there still something about her that only creeps like him could see? Had he seen the suffering little girl, who felt so rejected that she was pathetically eager for any father figure to love her? Laura was devastated by this thought. She felt the same loneliness and fear as she had when she had been unable to protect herself from her father's anger, from the beatings that no one deserved, and from the vicious name-calling. But most of all, she felt pure, unadulterated fury at the unfairness of it; the same rage she had felt as a child against her abusive father.

The safe world she built for herself at college—shored up by her plans, her goals, her carefully selected friends, and her achievements—began to tumble down around her. Her optimism was replaced by an anger that seemed so out of proportion to what happened to her that it scared her.

During the next few weeks, she began to drink more gin and vodka than usual, even though she knew she shouldn't. At first, it was just enough to take the edge off the anger. But alcohol or compulsive eating were the only things that dulled the pain, blocked out the memories, and drowned out the thoughts. They even calmed her rage. Compulsive eating, however, led to weight gain, so alcohol was her soother of choice. She bought the cheapest gin and vodka she could find and, attempting to avoid eating sugar, mixed it with sugar-free soda. It wasn't long before she was drinking every single day.

Laura soon realized that she had a problem. She was a bright, intuitive young woman. She knew exactly why she was drinking. She understood that her anger at Dr. Ice was related to her father. She knew that the drinking was interfering with her goals.

She had no money, but she needed help, and she sought it at the only place she knew—her college guidance counselor's office. She was sent to a free counseling service on campus, staffed by graduate PhD candidate students from a nearby university.

Laura walked into the counseling office at the appointed time and sat down. The young female therapist sat close to Laura to put her at ease and got right to the point.

"What prompts you to drink? What are you struggling with?"

Laura explained how her craving for alcohol increased after the incident in Dr. Ice's physics classroom, and she told the counselor the whole story. "When I think about Dr. Ice, I get extremely angry," she concluded. "But the anger isn't just at Dr. Ice. I become extremely angry at my father. I start thinking about Dr. Ice, and in a few minutes, I'm angry at my dad."

"Did your father ever abuse you?"

"No."

"Did your home have any abuse?"

"No, my home was just an average, normal home, like everybody else's."

"OK. Tell me some of the things you remember about home. What was it like?"

Laura began telling the counselor how it was in her house growing up—and soon she was explaining how her father beat her mother and the kids.

The counselor listened quietly. She didn't say a word, but her eyes got bigger and bigger. Finally, she said, "Laura, that is not normal! That is an abusive home!"

"Really?"

"Yes!"

"Well, I know he beat us, and he beat Mom, and I hated it; but I thought it was normal. I assumed that was the way every family lived!"

"Laura, did anyone ever sexually abuse you?"

Laura slowly shook her head. Just as she was about to say no, the memory of something pink covering her face suddenly filled her mind. She could feel the skirt of a pink dress being thrown over her head. She remembered how it felt not to be able to see and how confused and scared she was when her father told her to turn over and he climbed onto the bed on top of her.

She recounted this incident to the therapist, which was long buried but now as vivid in her mind as though it happened yesterday, and she relived how bewildered and frightened that little girl felt. The counselor said, "That was sexual abuse. Do you remember it ever happening again?"

Laura shook her head. "No, that was the only time I remember. From that time on, I was so afraid of my father that I became very good at staying out of his way. I ran whenever he came near me. I made sure I was never alone with him again. When I think of my father, I'm angry because of his cruelty, because of the beatings, and because of the things he said and how the whole family suffered at his hands. That happened to me or someone in my family almost every day until the kids got old enough to defend themselves."

Laura continued to see that counselor for the next several months until the end of her sophomore year. They talked about ways for Laura to handle her anger toward her father and her negative attitudes about men in general—aimed at helping her deal with her alcoholism and get through her day-to-day life. The student counselor had neither the time nor the experience to help Laura come to terms with her past. The counselor believed that a long-term psychoanalytic approach would help her, but the few remaining months of the school year weren't long enough to complete her recommended program of counseling. However, during one of their sessions, she said something that had a profound effect on Laura: "You will live to repeat what you grew up with unless you learn otherwise."

Laura took that statement to heart. She decided to do everything she could to learn otherwise. *I am going to read books on every topic that may have played a role in why things went so poorly in my home. I want to know what caused those problems.*

She was already experimenting with religion, going from church to church. She started studying about food, reading everything she could find on how the foods a person eats can help or hurt the body. She moved on to reading how religion can affect the family dynamic. She never left these topics entirely— just changed her focus from one aspect to another. She switched to psychology and read about family relationships and abuse. Then she read books on money management. "I have to read, learn, and understand what caused the problems in my home so that I never repeat them," she told herself again and again.

All of this reading would have long-term benefits, but it did nothing to help Laura's current problems. The drinking got worse. With her increased alcohol consumption, her health deteriorated. She worried that her once-damaged kidneys would fail again and ruin her plans for the future. She tried to compensate by consistently taking the doctor-recommended large amounts of mineral supplements. They seemed to help offset the effects of the alcohol and keep her from having kidney problems.

The anger, however, didn't go away. How Laura hated that helpless, sniveling inner child, always seeking love! The realization that her abusive childhood, her unavailable, sometimes cold and distant mother, and her angry, violent father were far from normal only made her anger worse. She tried to hold everything together and she succeeded, all the while maintaining the funny, lively, friendly, outgoing face that the world knew as Laura Sicking.

CHAPTER 11

....

Um, I'm Kinda Into Health Food

Grayson was a junior college. When her two years there were over, Laura made plans to transfer to Texas Tech University in Lubbock. In the meantime, she needed a place to stay and a good summer job. She moved to Dallas to live with Lois, who had invited her to share her small apartment in the city. Lois was single and was working as a nurse at Parkland Hospital.

Laura qualified for a Pell Grant for low-income students and was awarded a small engineering for women scholarship for the fall semester. She also lined up several college loans, but, to make ends meet, she still needed to make some good money. She came across a help-wanted ad in the *Dallas Morning News*. The Xerox Corporation was looking for assembly line workers for the summer. The job paid ten dollars an hour—very good pay for the time. The ad said interviews would be on Saturday morning from 8:00 A.M. to 12:00 P.M. *I've got to get that job!*

Dressed in her best, most professional-looking outfit, Laura arrived at the warehouse site in North Dallas at seven on Saturday morning, determined to be the first in line. There were already 298 people ahead of her. Laura stood in the hot Texas sun with the others, sweating in her suit. Every ten minutes the door opened, ten people were ushered inside, and the rest of the line inched forward.

Laura struck up a conversation with the two women next to her in line. They were both school teachers looking for summer work. "I have to get this job!" Laura told them breathlessly. "I'm a college student, paying my own way through, and I will run out of money if I don't get this job!"

The two women laughed. They took in her skinny, wiry body, her twitchy, barely contained energy, and her winning personality. "If anybody can cut in this line, you can!" one of them said.

"You know what?" Laura grinned. "I can!" She started watching the door, timing how often it opened.

At ten o'clock, someone opened the door, stepped outside, and made an announcement. "We have only forty positions to fill today. We will interview only the next 140 people. Everybody else can go home." The people at Laura's end of the line began to leave, but she started walking the opposite way, toward the front of the line, timing her pace so that she arrived just as the door opened to let in the next batch of ten applicants. But she didn't quite make it! The door shut right in her face.

Laura stayed right where she was at the head of the line. She looked around at the others waiting in line and shifted into full comedienne mode, laughing and telling jokes, one right after another. Soon many of those waiting were laughing with her. A tall black man stood next to her. She included him in the jokes, making eye contact, laughing and talking.

She had been standing there for only a few minutes when a skinny white man walked up from the back of the line.

"Hey, lady! Weren't you back there with us?"

"Yes, I was."

"Well, don't you think you ought to get back here where you belong?"

Laura grinned. "Actually, no, I don't!"

All of Laura's new friends laughed, closing ranks around her, and the man shook his head and walked back to his end of the line. The same thing happened again. It was a different white guy this time—one who was more serious. He appealed to the crowd, including the tall black man standing next to Laura, "Don't you all think she should go back to the end of the line where she belongs?"

The tall black guy took a step toward him. "Leave her alone!" he said. "She's with me." The white guy backed off, but he told the rest of the crowd about Laura's brazen maneuver as he moved back to his place, far down the line. A few minutes later the door opened, and the next group was ushered in, Laura included. As they walked through the door, her new black friend leaned down and whispered, "Don't feel bad. I cut in line too."

The group of ten who just made it through the door were told to line up again inside, and each one was assigned a number, given an application form, and told to fill it out as quickly as possible. As they found chairs and began to tackle the forms, the guy next to Laura glanced over and smiled at her. "Hi, I'm Tom," he said. "What number are you?" Laura held up her number. It was 108. Tom grinned. "I'm 107. What's your name?" Laura told him.

"I heard you out there in the line," he said. "You're pretty funny. You ought to be on television or something."

Laura looked up from the application form in her lap and smiled. "Thanks! I'm not always so pushy, it's just that I really need this job."

Tom nodded. "Yeah, me too," he said. The two continued to chat while they waited for their numbers to be called. Before Tom waved good-bye and his tall, wide-shouldered form disappeared down a corridor, he got her phone number.

Then it was Laura's turn to be interviewed. The man who spoke with her was another tall black man. "What time did you get up this morning to be here?" he asked with a laugh.

"Six o'clock."

"That late? How did you get in?"

Laura told him her story. "Wow, that's gutsy," he said.

"Yeah," Laura replied earnestly. "I know it wasn't right, but I knew if you could just meet me, you would want to hire me. I'm an engineering student. I make straight As. I'm from a poor farm family, and I need this job bad."

"You have engineering training?"

"Yes, two years."

"You shouldn't be competing with these people for an assembly line job. You should be interviewing for an engineering job." He escorted Laura personally to the right person in the engineering department, who interviewed and hired her on the spot. She had just landed a well-paying summer engineering job.

Laura had to leave by the same door through which she had entered and pass by all the people still waiting, who were now booing at her. "Did you get the job, lady?" somebody yelled.

Laura shook her head. "Nope," she said, putting on a sad face. "I didn't get it." And she didn't; not *that* job. She kept on walking down the line as the crowd jeered and nearly ran to her car before they could turn on her. *That was a dangerous thing to do*, she thought to herself as she got into her car and locked the doors. Desperation made her bold. *I'm not proud of what I just did. But I had to get that job so that I won't go hungry or have to drop out of college.*

Tom called her the next day and asked her out to dinner the following night. Tom was quite tall, at least six feet two inches tall, and good looking. He was very athletic and had a muscular build. His hair was dark, straight, and cut short; his skin was a smooth olive tone; and his eyes were warm and brown. As she welcomed him into her apartment, Laura felt again what impressed her most about him the day before—his air of easy self-confidence.

Their first date went well. Tom was easy to be with and was a great conversationalist. Laura enjoyed his company, and it wasn't long before the two were spending most of their free time together.

Tom was a premed student, soon to start his senior year at Northwestern University in Evanston, Illinois, a suburb of Chicago. His dad was a professor in Northwestern's chemistry department. Tom told her that his parents were conservative Catholics, although he had rejected most of the religion, much like Laura herself.

That summer the two of them went on many dates, but they never went to church together, although Laura continued to visit various Christian churches on her own. Yet, a part of Laura that longed for her family's love liked the idea that they would approve of Tom's Catholic background. They would also be pleased that he was going to be a doctor. Part of her couldn't imagine ever marrying someone without their acceptance, even while her adult self scoffed at the idea of marriage. But whenever she thought of her wedding, it was always in a Catholic Church. Of course, she told Tom very little about her family or her painful childhood and nothing at all about the incident with Dr. Ice.

Tom was a free spirit. Each summer he took a break from his studies and went somewhere for fun. One summer he rode his bicycle from Chicago to Florida. This summer he came to Dallas with a friend from school, just to hang out. He and Laura enjoyed long walks and picnics, concerts and dinners, and just hanging out with friends. They were falling in love.

Despite her newfound happiness, Laura continued to suffer from feelings of anger that summer and to struggle with alcohol. There was no counseling and no therapy available. She was determined not to let her inner turmoil interfere with her long-term goals. She sought her own coping mechanisms. Sometimes they helped, and sometimes they didn't. Spending time with Tom helped. Exercise helped too. Running always helped her deal with her anger and sadness by replacing them with the euphoria some people call a runner's high, but she couldn't run constantly. She had to find other ways to cope as well.

One afternoon she was driving the Vega home from her job at Xerox. While fiddling with the radio dial, she found the beautiful sounds of violins coming from the classical music station in Dallas. It was Strauss's "Blue Danube," and as she listened to it, she could feel her body and mind relaxing as the music filled her soul.

As soon as she could, she scoured local music stores and bought a marked-down album of Johann Strauss II's greatest hits—the first of what became a large collection of classical music.

She found in the music of the great composers another kind of therapy and a source of solace to help her cope. She listened to the classical station whenever she was in her car. She soon developed a list of favorite composers and bought discount records whenever she could find any.

Meanwhile, she continued to visit local churches and moved on to reading books about world religions. She found another way to cope when she came across something about yoga and meditation while reading a book on Buddhism that Joyce recommended. *Perhaps*, she thought, *yoga could help me gain control over my drinking and anger.* Laura knew nothing about yoga. She wasn't aware that there were many different types of yoga disciplines. To her, yoga was yoga, and she found a yoga class the way she found most things—in the Dallas Yellow Pages, and Joyce accompanied her on her first visit.

The class was taught by a slender, petite Indian woman. She had dark eyes and long straight, dark hair that was just beginning to go gray at the temples. Her manner was soft and gentle.

The yoga sessions lasted about an hour each time. The instructor gave every student a word to say. They were to close their eyes, empty their minds, and repeat the word, called a mantra, over and over as the trainer guided them through various yoga poses. Mantras are often the names of Hindu gods or goddesses, although Laura didn't know that at the time. She did notice that the names of some of the yoga poses included religious meanings; words such as *bowing* and *worshiping*. Laura found that the physical movements of yoga and the concentration it required helped to calm her mind.

Spending time with Tom, classical music, jogging, and yoga all helped—some of the time. Keeping herself very busy helped too.

But when she thought of her father or Dr. Ice, the anger returned. She was right back where she started, and only alcohol or compulsive eating provided her with relief.

Laura and Lois enjoyed living together, but they clashed occasionally over food. There were verbal exchanges about food that gave Laura a good understanding that her family members wouldn't accept her becoming a vegetarian, if she chose to do so.

That summer Laura spent some of her spare time in bookstores, as she was still striving to find the keys to a happy life, often reading an entire book through without leaving the store and without buying the book. She would have purchased them, but her extremely tight budget made it impossible.

Laura and Tom both dreaded the end of that summer. When she was with him, Laura was happy and life was great. Tom told her she was beautiful and smart. He thought so highly of her that she dared to believe she was everything he thought she was. He projected his own healthy self-esteem on her, and she basked in the positive atmosphere he created. Laura could tell that Tom was an emotionally healthy person. With Tom, she could relax, let down her guard a little, and be herself. She felt safe, accepted, and loved.

Summer was nearly over. It was a beautiful day in August, and the two of them were picnicking in the park. They took a slow walk around the lake, holding hands and talking about the future. Tom was returning to Chicago to finish his last year of premed. Laura was leaving for Texas Tech to pursue her chemical-engineering degree.

"You know how I feel about you, don't you, Laura?" Tom looked down at the blond curls he had come to love. "You know I love you and I want to marry you."

Laura's heart thrilled; but even as he said it, she knew it was impossible. She knew they wouldn't see each other again for a long time. Tom was facing an intense last year of college, and then, if he was accepted into medical school, another four years of grueling work and study, plus his internship and residency. He had excellent grades and high confidence that he would get into the medical school of his choice. Laura would need another three years to finish her own degree. Both agreed that they wouldn't get married until their education was completed.

Tom knew he wouldn't have time for a wife, or even for a girlfriend. He couldn't make any promises or enter into any obligations.

"I totally understand," Laura assured him. "Neither of us is in a position to get married."

Now, when their summer together was over, Tom brought up the subject again. "Laura, will you wait for me? I'm not asking you not to date. I want you to have fun; but we belong together, and someday we will be. Will you promise to wait?"

Laura didn't want to break up with Tom. He was the best thing that had ever happened to her. So, filled with love and sadness, she committed to him that she would wait and told him good-bye. They promised to write to each other faithfully.

When the summer was over, Laura set out to drive to Texas Tech. She was traveling alone, with all of her possessions packed into the little brown Vega. With Dallas growing ever smaller in her rearview mirror and seven hours of driving ahead of her, she needed a way to occupy her mind during the trip. Classical music played on the radio until there wasn't a signal. She used the time to do what she thought of as a self-assessment. It was an effort to improve her life as she started a new phase of her education.

For years—as far back as the near-suicide incident when she was only fourteen—Laura used the meticulous planning of her life and future as a coping mechanism. She continued to do it through her life. Who was she? What did she believe? What was her truth? As she headed west toward Lubbock, she looked at every part of her life thus far, analyzing each aspect. Was she happy with where she was? What should she change? How should she change it?

Laura thought first about her emotional state. Obviously, she was not happy with where she was emotionally. She was filled with anger, and it was still driving her to drink too much. She needed help—serious help. What could she do about it? She decided that the first thing she would do when she arrived at Texas Tech would be to get herself into the free counseling program that the university offered.

Next Laura thought about her health. She was doing quite well healthwise that summer, despite the drinking. She was learning how to prepare and eat healthy foods, avoiding white sugar, and continuing to take large-dose mineral supplements. She was exercising regularly, running for miles almost every day. Her regimen seemed to be working. Her kidneys were functioning well with this program. She felt good about her progress toward good health and vowed to continue doing what she was doing.

Laura considered her financial state. For the first time in her life, she could relax a little about her finances. She was pleased that she had received the scholarship, the Pell Grant, and a government student loan. In addition, she had borrowed money from her mother. By that time, Mary had saved a considerable amount of money and willingly loaned Laura money but at the going interest rate. In addition, Laura had earned and saved good money that summer. She was doing well financially as she began her junior year of college.

Then she thought about her social life and had to smile. Tom told her he wanted her to have fun and date. Except for him, she had little experience at dating. Her uncertainty on how well she could manage full-time college classes with part-time work caused her to be cautious about how she spent her free time, including dating. Her extremely hectic schedule at Grayson—taking eighteen or nineteen credit hours of classwork and striving to make all As, along with her many hours of waitressing—left her with little time to date. She decided this had to change. She would take fewer classes so that she would have more time to date. *I'm committed to Tom*, she thought, *but I need a life. I'm twenty years old. I want to have fun like other girls my age. I'm going to get out and meet people. I won't get serious with anybody, but I will date more.*

The next item on Laura's list was academics. She excelled in her studies at Grayson, getting almost all As, except for Dr. Ice's class, of course. With two years of college experience behind her, she was confident that she could have a social life and still maintain good grades. She decided she was happy with where she was academically.

Finally, she thought about her spiritual life. She continued to feel lost spiritually. She was still searching for a church that taught ideas she could use to guide her life and still hoping to find the God that she knew as a child, who could give her the happiness she once had. She nearly finished her plan to attend services at all the Christian denominations represented in the Yellow Pages. There were only a few more in Lubbock that she wanted to visit.

Thus far, nothing she heard in these churches met her basic qualifications; nothing compelled her to visit any one of them more than a couple of times. She decided to complete her visits to Christian churches within the next few months and then focus on the study of other world religions.

As the brown Vega sped on toward Lubbock through miles and miles of empty Texas land, Laura began to ponder religion more deeply. She had visited many churches, listened to a lot of preachers, and read stacks of religious books and literature. But she wasn't any closer to finding a belief system that worked for her. *What do I really believe?* she thought. *What do I know for sure? What is truth as I understand it to be?* She searched her soul for answers and came up with three things she was absolutely sure of.

First, she believed with absolute certainty that God exists. She didn't know His name or much about Him, but she experienced His presence as a small child. The certainty that He is real never left her. That conviction survived everything that happened to her.

Second, she believed God is good. He is always on her side. He is a great guy. As a kid, she knew that He was loving, kind, and fair. In her young life, where little else was fair, she clung to that belief, and it still sustained her.

Most of the Christian churches she had visited thus far believed in an ever-burning hell. Laura couldn't accept that a God who is just and fair would subject every sinner, regardless of his or her sins, to the same unending eternal damnation. That seemed crazy to her, and it was one of the beliefs that kept her from returning to any of the Christian churches she visited.

And third, she believed in natural, universal laws. Her study of science confirmed what she knew intuitively. There are laws of nature that cannot be broken without consequences. They apply to everyone, no matter who a person is. They are independent of time or location. Whether a person believes in them or not, he will reap the consequences of his choices. For instance, if someone eats too much, he will get fat. Jump off a cliff, and she will hit the bottom. If a person wants to have a happy life with the least amount of suffering, he has to play by the rules of universal laws.

So those three things—that God exists; that He is good and fair; and that the world is governed by natural, universal laws—formed the basis of what Laura believed. It wasn't much of a belief system, but it was honestly all she had. She wanted more. She wanted a truth she could live by and a belief system that would guide her actions and direct her future.

She resolved to continue her efforts to study every religion until she found something that met her basic qualifications and helped her achieve her goal of a happy life. She knew she needed to be very careful about the religious ideas she chose to live by because fallacious religious ideas played a significant role in her mother's suffering and had imprisoned her mother. Laura learned that error enslaves people. Because truth is the opposite of error, then truth should set one free. Her quest was to find a truth to live by. But what was that truth?

CHAPTER 12

············

"Hi, I'm Steve"

Mind if I sit here?" Laura glanced up from her lunch then looked again. The owner of that voice with a deep, slow Southern drawl was a tall, good-looking, well-built young man.

"No, I don't mind. Please join me," she said with a friendly smile. The stranger lowered his cafeteria tray to the table and said, "Hi, I'm Steve."

Laura had been at Texas Tech for only a few weeks, but already she was making friends. Steve was just the kind of person she was drawn to: handsome, athletic, and judging by his well-pressed slacks and expensive sweater, from a well-to-do family. They struck up a conversation, and Laura soon learned that he, too, was an engineering student, with a second major in business. He played lacrosse on the university team. The friendship grew rapidly from that first lunch, and it wasn't long before the two were dating regularly. Although she and Tom agreed to date other people, Laura left all mention of Steve out of her letters to Tom, and she never mentioned Tom to Steve. She didn't feel that it was necessary to discuss such things with either man.

Making friends was easy for Laura. Just as at Grayson, her outgoing, gregarious manner drew people to her. She was soon in the center of a lively group of smart, attractive engineering and premed students, who studied hard, made good grades, and had fun.

But the sparkling personality was only Laura's external face. She continued to drink, even though she signed up with a campus therapist and started counseling sessions almost as soon as she arrived at the university. Although she wasn't aware of it, Laura still kept many of her emotions frozen in order to shield herself from the pain of her hurting inner child and to become a strong, successful adult. An experience involving her friend Gina brought this situation forcefully home to her.

Gina was lovely. She was petite and soft spoken, with big brown eyes behind round glasses and a serene face that formed a perfect oval. Laura was drawn to Gina because of her obvious intelligence, and the more she got to know this fine young woman, the deeper their friendship became. Gina's family was wealthy, and she was very close to her parents, who were staunch Southern Baptists.

Laura learned that Gina's mother had been fighting cancer for several years. They were friends for about four months when word came that Gina's mother had died. Gina was devastated, and her closest friends, Laura included, were gathering in her dorm room to help her cope with this terrible news.

Laura walked down the hall and entered the room full of sobbing young women. Two girls were sitting on the bed with Gina. Their arms were around her shaking shoulders, and their tears were mingling with hers. Other girls were also weeping openly, and their hands were full of soggy tissues. Quietly, Laura took a seat and looked around the room. Was this how she was supposed to act? She tried her hardest to identify with her grieving friend, but she felt nothing— no sadness, no sympathy, and no tears—nothing.

This lack of feeling took her by surprise. She, the young woman who placed compassion high on her list of attributes when choosing her friends, had none for her friend. *Something is really wrong with me*, she thought. *I don't know how I got this way. I'm not like other women. If my mother died tomorrow, I wouldn't cry. If my father died, I would feel nothing. I need to do something about it!*

She slipped out of Gina's room and returned to her own room. Pouring herself a drink, she thought about the whole experience. Why was she so devoid of feelings? Why couldn't she cry like all the other women? Then she remembered that when she was fourteen, she had told herself never to cry again. Well, she had been very successful at that—too successful. She thought about all of the events in her life that had led to her childhood decision never to cry.

At her next counseling session, she told the therapist about this experience. "I know I wouldn't cry if my mother died," she said. As they discussed the situation, a scene appeared in her mind, almost as if a video started to play inside her head.

As she watched the "video," she saw a tiny blond girl who was frantically crawling under a bed, screaming and fighting to get away from a big man who was trying to grab her. They were in a large room with two double beds. The man had something that looked like a pole. As Laura watched the scene, the child scrambled to one side, and the man ran around to the other, poked at her with the pole, and grabbed at her again.

It seemed to Laura as though this scenario went on for hours as the man chased the child back and forth. Then Laura was seized with panic and felt as though she was going to die. She was feeling the child's terror and knew, without a doubt, that she was that little girl. Although she had no idea who the man was, she believed she was reliving an incident that had happened to her. What was it?

As soon as she could, Laura called her mother and asked her about the memory. "Oh, yes, of course, I remember that," her mother said. "That was when your father had his first mental breakdown. You were about two and a half. Dad was hallucinating. He thought the Japanese were invading the country. He believed he needed to get all the children into one room to protect them. I didn't know what to do. I stayed in the room with all of the other children to keep them calm, and I hoped that you would come into that room too. You ran away to the girls' bedroom and hid under one of the beds! Your father got a broom and tried to poke you out. When that didn't work, he tried sitting on the bed, hoping his weight would flatten you and force you out. But it didn't. You stayed right where you were, in the farthest corner under the bed. Finally, he gave up and left you there."

Listening to her mother's words, Laura remembered exactly how she had felt, hiding alone under that bed, helpless and abandoned. She screamed and screamed for her mother, but she never came. There was no rescue. She was all alone, fighting for her life. Was that when the feelings of abandonment and negative feelings toward her mother started? Was that why she was unable to feel compassion for Gina when her mother died?

The therapist, a graduate student, did her best to help Laura deal with her feelings toward both her parents. She helped Laura understand that she felt abandoned by her mother because her mother hadn't been able to protect her from her father. She hated her father for his cruelty and transferred those feelings to men in general. Men were bad unless they were just friends. Friends were like brothers, and brothers were great. She loved her three little brothers.

Gina invited Laura to go to church with her, and she enjoyed it. She loved discussing religion with Gina, who was quite evangelistic about sharing her Southern Baptist faith. Sensing Laura's interest, Gina would get quite animated, preaching her church's doctrines with fervor. One day during one of these lively sessions, Gina got on the topic of hell. She assured Laura that Southern Baptists believe that sinners will burn in hell forever.

"That's baloney!" Laura's opinion on this subject hadn't changed a bit. "I don't believe that at all."

"But the Bible says so!" Gina countered emphatically.

Having been raised a conservative Catholic, Laura knew almost nothing about what the Bible contained, so she had no idea whether that was what it said or not. "Well," she told Gina, "if that's what the Bible says, then I don't believe in the Bible!"

"If you don't believe in the Bible, how can you believe in Jesus?" Gina asked.

Laura sobered immediately. "That's a very good question," she said slowly. "I guess I don't believe in Him either."

Gina didn't pull her punches. "Then you're not a Christian!" she responded.

"That's true," said Laura, suddenly realizing that fact for the first time. "I guess I'm not."

From that point onward, Laura abandoned the study of Christianity altogether and changed her focus to other world religions. There weren't a lot of opportunities near Lubbock, Texas, to observe Hindu, Buddhist, or Muslim worshipers, so she did her learning through books. Somehow, it didn't occur to her at this point to read the Bible for herself and find out what it really said. The only advantage of this was that when she finally did begin to study the Bible on her own, she was able to compare its truths to the other teachings she had studied previously.

As her university education progressed, Laura's trips home became less frequent because she was attending a school so far away, but she still went home to Muenster for Thanksgiving and Christmas.

She noticed something interesting was happening as her older siblings grew up and moved away. None of the kids visited their parents alone. They still turned up at holidays, but they checked with each other to coordinate their arrival and departure times. Once the children were able to leave home permanently and support themselves, none of them spent the night in the family home. Laura had learned enough by now to realize that other people's families didn't avoid and dread going home the way she and her siblings seemed to. Yet, something drew them together. Was it obligation? Or was it a longing for something they never had?

It wasn't conversation. The family found little to talk about when they were together. Surrounded by the very walls where so much suffering had happened, the memories came flooding back, but they were not shared. The wall of silence prevailed as it always had, and the talk was confined to education, politics, and other impersonal topics.

Laura's bright, educated siblings could confidently discuss current events on the world stage, but they couldn't share much of themselves with each other. Even "How are you doing?" was such a loaded question that it was not asked. There were no private, intimate, one-on-one conversations.

Laura felt invisible at these gatherings. She wanted to do the "normal" thing and visit her family during the holidays. She pictured a loving family with a caring mother and father—a place where she belonged. But for her, that family didn't exist. Her siblings may have felt the same way, but she didn't know.

She could walk into the Sicking living room at these gatherings and not be acknowledged by anyone. She could leave and not hear anyone say good-bye. Laura puzzled over this. Did her family members really not care, or were they as unable to reveal themselves as she was? It wasn't normal at all. It was empty.

The food at the Sicking family gatherings, as usual, was heavy, German, and pork laden. Virginia normally did most of the cooking. Laura found it difficult to stick to her new, healthier diet when she went home. She tried hard not to be obvious about it; in fact, she hid it from her family as long as she could. Because there were so few things she could eat, she brought her own food.

It wasn't long after a trip home to visit the family that Laura learned something surprising. Joan, a chemist, brought her testing equipment home with her and tested the family's drinking water. She found that the water had high levels of nitrates and nitrites. These chemicals come from urine—both animal and human. With the presence of urine also comes the possibility of parasites and bacterial contamination.

The Sickings' well was dug down five hundred feet to reach the nearest aquifer. The pens for their four hundred pigs, however, completely surrounded the well. It was obvious from Joan's testing that pig urine was seeping into the soil, all the way down to the aquifer that fed the well. She talked to her parents immediately and told them how badly contaminated the water was. "You need to move those pigs!" she said, and to their credit, they did.

When Laura learned about this, she wondered if her health problems were at least partially caused by contaminated water. For that matter, how many of her siblings' sicknesses, and even those of her parents, were due to this contamination? She was glad to know those pigs were moved, but the possibility existed that she still carried parasites and other contaminants in her body.

Back at school, Laura's relationship with Steve was progressing faster than she really wanted it to. Even though she still honored her commitment to Tom, she found herself falling for Steve, despite the fact that he was a devout Southern Baptist, as almost everybody on Texas Tech's campus was. On the plus side, he was a good man, committed to his faith, and good with money. She knew that above all, he wanted a home of his own with a wife and children. Laura happily went to church with him every Sunday. Steve had a gorgeous car and took her to expensive places. He bought her lavish gifts and escorted her to his fraternity's ball. She thought the world of Steve and loved the feeling of belonging it gave her to be part of a couple.

Laura knew that Steve was attracted to the accomplished young woman she had become, but she was convinced that he would find her weak, needy inner child pathetic and disgusting if she ever revealed that part of herself to him. She told him very little about her family, never revealing the wretchedness of the home she grew up in. She figured the less Steve knew about that, the better.

LIFE IN THE VALLEY

About nine months into their relationship, Steve began pressuring her to marry him. Laura found herself facing a dilemma. She knew that her family would oppose her marriage to Steve, and she wasn't sure she wanted to break her commitment to Tom and marry Steve, but she didn't want to be alone either. In the end, she let herself be coerced into an engagement.

During this time, she was taking an elective class called Communication in Relationships and Marriage. The professor presented a list of criteria for judging a possible mate based on statistical studies. Laura loved this list. It was right down her alley. The logic of it appealed to her analytical mind. The guidelines recommended that the criteria to judge potential spouses be in three categories, designated Types A, B, and C. A was the most influential, and C was the least. The suggested criteria reflected the fundamentalist, Southern Baptist character of Texas Tech. It included such questions as, do you belong to the same religion? Do you both attend church regularly? These were weighted heavily, and the right answer would go a long way toward scoring a candidate highly.

Other questions of high value included the following: Are your ages within five years of each other? Is there a premarital pregnancy? There were less weighty questions, such as education, socioeconomic status, and even the distance you would live from your in-laws. Laura used these questions to develop a personal scoring test that she used to rate any potential spouses.

Laura rated Tom, and he failed to meet the test's criteria for a successful life partner. Of course, Tom wasn't there. By this time, he had been accepted to several medical schools and chosen a school in Rome. Although they were still connected by their letters, he was thousands of miles away. So she decided to rate Steve. He failed too. In fact, his score was much lower than Tom's. But she proceeded with their relationship anyway.

Yet, Laura was uncertain about her future. She needed more information. She had consulted a psychic in the past, and now it seemed an appropriate time to do so again. She checked the local newspaper and found a small ad: "Have your fortune read for $10!" Laura looked up the address and made an appointment.

The house was a well-kept little bungalow in a fairly new suburban neighborhood on the edge of the town. A discreet sign in the window identified it as the residence of a psychic. The woman who answered the door was small in stature. Her long graying hair was parted in the middle and framed a slender face, with a rather long, pointed nose and eyes that were dark and piercing. She greeted Laura in a businesslike way, accepted her ten dollars, and invited her into the dining room, where the two women took chairs facing each other across the table.

There was nothing spooky or threatening about the situation. Laura sat down, feeling perfectly comfortable and looking forward to what she might learn.

She saw nothing wrong with psychics. In her Catholic frame of reference, they were merely people who had the ability to consult the dead who went to heaven. She thought of visiting a psychic as a method of obtaining information about the future that wasn't available any other way. Lots of people did it for fun. She was there to satisfy her curiosity. She was smart enough to be skeptical about the accuracy of any information she might receive, but she had no concept of the involvement of demons or of the dangers of the occult.

Laura brought a list of questions she prepared. She wanted to know about her future with Steve and what was going to happen when she graduated from college.

"Am I going to be happy with Steve?" she asked.

The psychic consulted the tea leaves in the saucer in front of her. Then she looked at Laura, and her voice was emphatic. "You're not going to marry Steve," she said. "You're going to break up."

This prediction upset Laura, so she changed the subject and asked a question about her family. The psychic told her detailed information about a certain family member and his life choices that half of the family didn't know about, but Laura knew. Laura was shocked that the psychic knew such detailed information and asked, "How do you know that?"

"Your guide is telling me."

Laura had read a great deal about black magic, witchcraft, and fortune-telling. She knew that spirit guides were considered to be the spirits of the dead. She also read that a medium or psychic did not easily make contact with a spirit guide; it was a right the medium had to earn.

"Can you see him?" Laura asked.

The psychic nodded. "Yes."

"Can you hear him?" she asked again.

Again, the psychic nodded. "Yes."

Laura had read that such a high level of communication with a spirit guide required a great deal of preparation on the part of the medium. "What did you do to earn that right?" was her next question.

"I pray six hours a day."

That'll do it, Laura thought. She noticed that the medium did not say to whom she prayed.

The psychic continued to tell Laura about her future. She told her that she would have several more boyfriends, but that she wouldn't marry any of them.

Laura found the visit upsetting. She didn't get the answers she wanted, and she was confused and perplexed by the psychic's knowledge of family members that very few people knew about. There was something about the whole thing that unsettled her. She determined that she would return in a year and ask the psychic the same questions. Would her answers change, or would they remain the same? Despite her misgivings, she eventually returned to that psychic two more times.

Meanwhile, Steve insisted that she meet his family, so they drove home one weekend to Odessa, Texas, which was several hours away. His family was nice, and Laura dazzled them with her outgoing, sparkling personality.

A month before spring break, they finally got engaged. Steve gave her a beautiful but simple engagement ring and began a campaign to get her to marry him right away. Almost as soon as the ring was on her finger, Laura began suffering from stomach pains. She took Maalox and other antacids and tried to ignore this warning sign. When Steve urged an early wedding, Laura hemmed and hawed.

"I want to finish college, Steve! I have another two and a half years to go. Let's put it off until then." She was really doing whatever she could to prolong the engagement. Part of her still didn't want to get married at all and couldn't even imagine herself ever being married to Steve.

Steve kept up the pressure. Laura tried another tactic. "You know I'm a Catholic, Steve. You're going to have to become a Catholic! If I marry a Southern Baptist, my family will disown me. You're going to have to convert!" Steve deflected this argument by never giving Laura a straight answer. She let it drop.

Steve wanted to meet Laura's family and began insisting that they make the trip to Muenster together. Laura put him off as long as she could, but when spring break rolled around, they drove to Muenster. Laura didn't prepare her family for Steve—and neither did she prepare Steve for her family. Not surprisingly, the visits with Laura's siblings and parents went very poorly. Several family members told derogatory jokes about Protestants, indicating that the family held strong prejudices. Steve broke up with her the next day, as soon as they arrived back at Texas Tech. It wasn't pretty. "I can't handle your family," he told her.

"I'm sorry that you feel that way," she told him, but she wasn't surprised at all. Laura gave the ring back, and within an hour, she was free of stomach pain. No more Maalox. She had been engaged for about a month.

Depression set in after the breakup. Laura's ego was bruised. But more than that, she missed Steve. She loved him, at least, as she understood love to be. And Steve was right about one thing—it would take an extremely strong and wise man to accept her family. *I'm not going to marry a Catholic, you can bet on that, but how could any non-Catholic man ever deal with meeting my family? Maybe, if I could just get him past the initial shock, I could promise him that we would visit them very infrequently,* she reasoned.

Then she sank even deeper into despair. *If a man found out very much about my background at all, he wouldn't want to marry me anyway, never mind meeting my family.*

No, she thought as she was filled with sadness. *No man would ever love me if he knew my secrets. How could he?* It was many years before she was able to share the secrets of her childhood with anyone.

CHAPTER 13

....

That's a Bunch of Hooey!

L aura wallowed in her misery for several months. Her innate resilience and her ability to analyze her situation gradually allowed her to come to terms with the loss of Steve and to move on with her life.

She redoubled her efforts to improve herself and find happiness in her life. Since the conversation she had had with Gina and the realization that she wasn't a Christian, she focused her reading on the investigation of other world religions, such as Islam, Hinduism, and Buddhism, and scoured the university's library for every book available on these subjects.

With no one to guide her, she delved into what were often huge volumes, drawing out bits and pieces of information, sometimes in no particular order but more often in a systematic way. She began by reading a biography of the religion's founder. Then she read that religion's sacred writings, and books that discussed its doctrines, beliefs, and practices.

There was a major obstacle in Laura's plan to find the "right" religion. She began to realize it while researching Christianity, and she came to understand it better as she learned more about other world religions. Every religion, every denomination, every church, every sect, and every offshoot of a sect believed they had the "truth"—all of them. How could she study each one's sacred writings and make an objective judgment about whether what she was reading was truth or not? She couldn't. Many times she would ask herself, after reading a religion's sacred writings or a list of its doctrines, *How can I know objectively that this is truth?* She could never answer that question for herself. As a result, she could not accept any sacred writings or religious doctrines.

She realized that it was unquestioning faith that led people to accept certain concepts or doctrines as truth. Regardless of whether they had the truth, some truth, or no truth, faith was what kept them believing in their religion. While she still believed in God, she lost her faith in the German Catholic Church of her childhood, in Christianity, and in religion in general because she could no longer accept beliefs in an unquestioning manner. She needed to have an objective way of answering her question about truth. Thus far, no church, denomination, or religion could answer that question.

Deep down inside, Laura was a skeptic. She developed a distrust of all religion. Despite her skepticism, the joy and happiness she experienced with God as a child compelled her to continue her search for truth. She still believed it could be found, but that it was like a needle in a haystack. She could find it only if she searched with all her heart.

She started with Islam. She didn't get very far with the Koran, however, and soon gave up on it. She read something at random in one of her library books that indicated the erroneous belief that Islam was the only world religion that taught women have no souls. If a Muslim man kills his wife, according to the book, it isn't murder because she has no soul. That idea, whether true of all Muslims or not, offended her so completely that she stopped her study of Islam at once. It was too similar to what she knew of traditional European Catholicism's oppressive views toward women.

She found Hinduism more interesting. She was intrigued by the idea of karma and curious about reincarnation and the caste system. She was put off, however, by the concept of thousands of gods and goddesses and the idea that anybody could become a god. There was a god of war, a god of peace, another one for fertility, a god of harvest—a god for everything a person could think of. Laura was reminded again of the Catholic faith she grew up in, where there were different saints to pray to for different things, such as women praying to Saint Teresa if they wanted to have a baby or seeking the intercession of Saint Christopher for safety when traveling. As a young adult, she thought that praying to saints made no sense, and that opinion hadn't changed.

She came across a story in one of the books she read on Hinduism that stated India uses 15 percent of its gross national product to feed sacred rats in a temple. The story went on to explain that one of the Hindu goddesses was supposed to be reincarnated as a rat. *Feeding rats? This is irrational*, she thought, *when there are so many starving people in India, but perhaps it makes sense to them when viewed in the context of their doctrine of karma.* However, weren't people more important than rats?

Then she got to Buddhism and found, to her surprise, that she liked it. She was impressed with the Buddhist lifestyle and writings. The essences of Buddha's teachings are in the four noble truths that state suffering exists; it has a cause; it has an end; and there is a way to bring suffering to an end. In Buddhism, desire and ignorance lie at the root of suffering. Laura agreed with these basic ideas. Her desire for alcohol brought her a lot of suffering. Ignorance played a major role in the erroneous ideas that caused the suffering in her home and her childhood. In Laura's mind, because knowledge fights ignorance, then it can fight suffering. All this made sense. She also thought the doctrine of reincarnation made a lot more sense than burning in hell forever.

According to Buddhism, the way to end suffering included having the right understanding, thoughts, speech, actions, livelihood, efforts, mindfulness, and concentration. Laura knew her mind was filled with too many negative thoughts, and they were destructive. Hatred, resentment, jealousy, and envy—these were negative thoughts. Love, joy, kindness, and goodness—these were the positive thoughts that must replace negativity. But how was she to get rid of her negative thoughts?

She also liked Buddhism's emphasis on vegetarianism. She was already leaning in that direction. Her experiences on the farm ensured that. There was a great deal about vegetarianism in what she read. She learned that there are eight levels of vegetarianism. She absorbed new terms, such as *lacto-ovo vegetarian, macrobiotics,* and *vegan.* Buddhists were big on the sacredness of life and believed that everything had a soul, including plants. Laura learned from her reading that she could eat a cucumber because the plant would give it to her freely. But she couldn't eat a cabbage or a carrot, because she would have to kill the plant, thus destroying its soul.

Laura looked up from her reading when she got to this part. *That's a bunch of hooey*, she thought. However, she decided it was time to become a vegetarian. She was eating only chicken and turkey anyway. But becoming a vegetarian was harder than she thought. She had no idea how to cook vegetarian meals for herself.

The final thing she gained from her study of Buddhism and the life story of its founder, Siddhartha Gautama, was the conviction that truth is very, very important. Truth had to guide one's life. And what was the truth?

About this time, Joyce sent her a book called *Sugar Blues* by William Dufty. It was a breakthrough bestseller on all the research that was done up to that time on white sugar (sucrose). It made a persuasive case that refined sugar was an addictive drug and very harmful to the human body. Laura knew that sugar was bad for her, and she was doing her best to eliminate it from her diet. But up to that point, she hadn't realized just how bad it really was.

About two-thirds of the way through *Sugar Blues*, Laura resolved to stop eating everything containing white sugar and to do it cold turkey that very day, even though the book advised against such a drastic step. By that evening, she was running a fever.

The next morning she woke up too sick and weak to attend her classes. Laura ate a bowl of sugary cold cereal and felt well enough to go to her classes.

A more gradual withdrawal from sugar met with better success, and soon Laura was transitioning to a sugar-free diet. She felt much better and was convinced that sugar is poison! She tried to eliminate it from her diet altogether.

This was easier said than done. Laura still hadn't learned how to cook. She needed to learn how to prepare healthy, sugar-free meals for herself. It took her three years, but she succeeded in eliminating white sugar from her diet entirely. She didn't buy or eat anything with white sugar in it.

Then she received another box of books from Joyce and came across a slim volume inside called *Steps to Christ.* Although she had given up entirely on Christianity, she still followed her plan to read every book she received from cover to cover. Joyce, who by this time was an avid Southern Baptist, told her she especially liked this book. "I buy them by the carton," Joyce wrote. "I give them away to everybody I meet."

Although this book was less than a hundred pages long, Laura just couldn't get through it. She couldn't handle a book about Christ. It was the wrong time in her life for such a book. She couldn't put it on her bookshelf; that was only for books she had read all the way through and agreed with. But she couldn't bring herself to throw it away or trade it in at the used bookstore either. Finally, she stuck it in the glove box of the Vega, thinking, *Out of sight, out of mind.*

That August, she met Phillip, a fellow engineering student. This relationship started when he sat down beside her in the cafeteria. Phillip was no Adonis. He lacked Tom's or Steve's impressive physical attributes. Short and dark haired, he was not particularly outgoing or friendly or debonair or athletic. Laura was attracted to him because of his superior mind. Phillip had no religion at all. Like Laura, he was a skeptic. The two of them drifted into a relationship and ended up dating for most of a year. Phillip, like Steve, had plenty of money, and Laura enjoyed the fancy restaurants, the fraternity balls, and the nice car. She used her scoring test to rate Phillip, and, like Steve, he failed; but still she kept seeing him.

Then spring came, and Phillip began to pressure Laura to marry him. Once again Laura was filled with conflict. She was still writing to Tom, and as far as he knew, they were still committed to waiting for each other. She didn't know her own mind. What should she do? She went to see the psychic again.

"You are not going to marry this man," the little woman with the long gray hair and the piercing dark eyes told her. "There will be several more men in your life before you meet the one you will marry."

Laura finally gave in and allowed Phillip to give her an engagement ring. Almost immediately, the terrible stomach pains returned and out came the Maalox again, although the chalky-white liquid did little to stop the agony. Laura broke up with Phillip the next day and was cured within the hour. It was then that she woke up to the connection between her engagements and the excruciating stomach pain she experienced with each one. Laura longed to have a husband to share her life with someday, but obviously, something was holding her back. *I'm going to have to get to the bottom of this problem*, she thought, *if I'm ever going to have a decent relationship with a man.*

Something else that affected Laura's thinking happened during that year. It occurred in a class in thermodynamics. This subject, required for her chemical-engineering major, involved those aspects of physics that dealt with the relationships between heat and other forms of energy or power. Thermodynamic principles are used everywhere—in car engines, in power plants, even in the refrigerator at home.

The professor outlined the four laws of thermodynamics, which are absolute rules that everything in the universe is affected by and obeys. In the world of science, something is defined as a law if it can be duplicated in a laboratory setting; in other words, it can be verified over and over again. It never changes, as opposed to a theory, which can't be duplicated or verified in a lab. Laws in science are always superior to theories. This idea resonated with Laura. She believed that the universe was governed by natural laws—laws that never changed. She listened even more carefully.

The professor was stating the second law of thermodynamics; it says that the measure of entropy (or chaos) is always increasing. In other words, everything in the universe is moving from order to chaos.

As soon as the professor made that statement, Laura saw an instant conflict between that law and the theory of evolution, which states just the opposite—that order was formed out of chaos.

Laura was taught evolution in her Catholic school catechism classes and in her college courses and saw no reason to dispute it. But now she had a question. She raised her hand.

"Professor, there's a problem here," she began. "Either the second law of thermodynamics is wrong or the theory of evolution is wrong."

Immediately, the class went into an uproar. The seventy-five or so students in the room (only five of whom were female, incidentally) began to scoff. "Come on! You have to believe this stuff!" someone shot out.

"I don't have to believe anything!" Laura shot back. "Evolution says that life began out of chaos, and that everything evolved from that chaos to the order we see today. This law of thermodynamics states that there was order to start with, and that it is gradually evolving to chaos. So which is it? It can't be both!" Pandemonium still reigned as students argued with Laura and with each other.

The instructor stepped in. "Calm down," he said to the class. "She's correct. There is a conflict." Then he turned and addressed Laura directly. "Maybe what was happening when evolution was taking place on our planet for millions of years is that things were going crazy, and there was disorder throughout the universe so that the overall balance was to disorder," he said.

Laura thought that explanation was pretty lame. "But we don't know what was going on in the rest of the universe. All we know is what was happening on earth. So I really don't think you can come up with an explanation that includes the rest of the universe in the equation," she replied.

The professor shrugged his shoulders and acknowledged that he couldn't explain the conflict between the theory of evolution and the second law of thermodynamics. Right then and there, Laura decided that, for her, the theory of evolution was off the table. It was not true or incomplete, at best.

Laura, the seeker of truth, just happened to come upon this bit of truth. For her, it had nothing to do with religion. At that point, she had not heard the Creation story; she simply rejected evolution as false, and she did it on a purely scientific basis. Rejecting the theory of evolution and everything that went with it was a big step for someone who loves science.

CHAPTER 14

....

"You Don't Belong Here!"

I t was Christmas of 1980, and Laura had a new problem. Switching her major in midstream had cost her. Some of the classes she took as a premed major didn't transfer into her new field. It was taking her five years to finish her chemical-engineering degree—not four.

The cash she earned the previous summer took her through the first semester; but as she faced the second, she had only two hundred dollars to her name. That wasn't enough for her tuition, much less her dormitory fees or books. She needed a thousand dollars to finish her education and get her degree. She planned to extend her government-sponsored, low-income based Pell Grant for one more year. She filled out an application for another Pell Grant, only to be disqualified. Her grants and scholarships, she learned, were based on the assumption that she would finish in four years. Now the money had dried up, and she was broke.

She tried borrowing from the university but ran into the same problem. Their loans were based on a four-year program. She went to the bank in Muenster but couldn't provide the collateral they required for a loan. In desperation, she asked her mother for help, although she already owed her more than six thousand dollars. Laura's mom refused. She noticed that Laura had recently purchased a new suit, which she needed for job interviews, and concluded that she was wasting her money.

Laura spent her entire Christmas vacation in Lubbock, pounding the pavement, looking for a job. Nobody would hire her once they learned she was only a semester away from graduation. She was desperate.

With no idea how she would pay her bills, Laura enrolled in school for her final semester, using her last two hundred dollars to buy her books. The university sent her a statement for her tuition, room, and board. With this bill in hand, she went to the counseling office and asked for help.

"You need to see the director of financial aid," she was told. "If anybody can help you, he would be the one."

She went to the financial aid director and pleaded her case. He was sympathetic but didn't offer much hope. She pleaded some more. "Well," he finally said with a sigh, "give me two weeks. Let me see what I can do." Laura left his office feeling dejected. The situation looked hopeless.

Two weeks later she returned to his office. He met her at the door with a big smile on his face. "Laura, you are one lucky young woman. Just this past week, the Texas legislature voted to extend Pell Grant eligibility to fifth-year students as long as they are going to school full time and will graduate at the end of their fifth year. No new grants were awarded this semester; but since you previously submitted your paperwork, your Pell Grant was approved. You got in under the wire." Then he handed her an envelope. Inside was a check for fourteen hundred dollars.

Laura was so relieved that she nearly hugged the financial aid director. Instead, she thanked him and left his office feeling like she was walking on air. With her financial worries gone, she plunged into her final semester and began looking for a job in California.

When spring break came, Laura went back to Dallas to spend the holiday with Joan, Virginia, and Lois. It was her habit to attend the yoga class whenever she was in town, going to the same teacher she had found three years before. One day, while her sisters were working, she went to the class by herself. As she walked into the room, there were about eight students already doing yoga.

She took her place on a mat, began doing yoga while repeating her mantra, and attempted to empty her mind, as she was taught.

As she meditated while doing yoga, an image formed in her mind. She saw a pair of large double doors in the distance, surrounded by clouds. The doors opened, and soft light streamed out. A blond woman came through the doors and walked slowly toward her. As she drew nearer, Laura recognized the woman as herself. The woman began to speak. "I will tell you what truth is."

Laura gasped. Truth was extremely important to her. Truth was what she sought—what she spent her life searching for, and what seemed to elude her.

The woman continued to speak. "This is truth. Truth is the sum of your experiences. Truth comes from your thoughts, feelings, and senses. It is what you feel. It is what you can see and touch."

Laura completely rejected that idea. *That's not the way to find truth*, she thought. *Truth involves the mind, not merely the senses.* The experience made her very uncomfortable, and she got up from her place on the mat to speak to the guru and tell her what she saw.

The teacher clapped her hands and smiled. "Oh, you just reached the second level of enlightenment, Laura! Very few Americans ever reach the second level. You are very special. This means that you are holy. You will reach all eight levels of enlightenment and become a goddess!" When Laura heard this, she thought, *I know what holy is—and I know it isn't me. I will never become god.*

Laura thanked the guru and immediately gathered up her belongings and left the room. *I'm out of here*, she thought. *I want nothing to do with this—ever again.* Later, as she learned more about the many different types of yoga disciplines, Laura realized that she had inadvertently found her way into a yoga class whose teacher focused on Buddhist spiritual practices as well as yoga exercise and movements. She wanted to have nothing further to do with Buddhism, and that was her last yoga class.

Back at college to begin the last semester of their fifth and final year, Laura's friend Melissa was feeling restive and uncertain. She wanted a degree that matched her natural talents, but her father wanted her to be an engineer. "I'm so sick of chemical-engineering classes," she confided to Laura one night at the beginning of the semester when they were looking at their schedules together. "Besides, one of my chemical-engineering professors, Dr. Clement, discouraged me in my attempt to become an engineer. He told me I have the brains but not the personality for it, whatever that means! I think I'm going to switch my major to something completely different—something I really enjoy, such as English, Spanish, or art."

"That's crazy, Melissa! You have so much invested in chemical engineering! You're so close!"

"Yeah, but I'm just fed up." Melissa's round face looked glum as she sat cross-legged on the bed. "I tell you, I simply cannot face another chemical-engineering class, particularly one with Dr. Clement."

"Fine, but promise me you'll talk to the admissions office before you do anything drastic. There might be a way to change your degree and still use the credits you already have," Laura pleaded.

Melissa reluctantly agreed, and the next time Laura saw her, her whole attitude had changed. "You're not going to believe this," she said as her face was transformed by a happy smile. "I changed my degree from a bachelor of science in chemical engineering to a bachelor of arts in chemical engineering. Who knew that was even possible? I already have enough classes for my degree. I can finish out this semester with Spanish, art, and music—whatever liberal arts I want. Thanks, Laura! If you hadn't stopped me, I would never have known that. I would have thrown it all away!"

Laura was happy for her friend. She knew Melissa needed a marketable degree and one that could help her earn a good salary. Laura was glad she was able to help

Melissa stay on track. For the first time in her life, she experienced the joy that comes from helping someone else, and she really liked the feeling. She realized that she would like to experience the joy of helping others more in her life.

Laura's last visit to the psychic in Lubbock occurred toward the end of that last semester, shortly before she graduated from Texas Tech. She had just broken up with her latest boyfriend, another Steve. This Steve also pressured her to marry him, just as her previous boyfriends had. She agreed, and the stomach pain came back. Now she was free. No more Steve, and no more pain. She accepted a job in California, and Steve accepted one in Texas.

She was looking forward to fulfilling her dream and moving to California after graduation. She had lots of decisions to make in the next few months. She was excited about what her future might hold. Her curiosity drew her one more time to the psychic.

The psychic received her again, ushering her into the same dining room and taking a seat across the table from her. Although the woman was never particularly friendly, this time Laura sensed, for no apparent reason, a distinctly hostile attitude. She took Laura's money, and Laura began her questions about her future.

"I see the man you are going to marry," the psychic said, peering at her tea leaves. "He is tall and slender, with auburn hair."

Hmm, thought Laura. *That's interesting. I don't even know any men with auburn hair.*

"I see you being married in a chapel."

What? thought Laura. *Catholics don't get married in a* chapel! Only Protestants used the word in that sense. This psychic was telling Laura that she would not be married in a Catholic church and that she would have a Protestant wedding. Laura had visited the churches of every Protestant denomination she could find, and none of them had doctrines she could accept. She could not imagine herself getting married in any of them. That seemed to be just plain unrealistic.

"I'm not getting married in a chapel. I would be disowned by my family if I did!"

The piercing, dark eyes bored into Laura's face. "Believe me," she said, "you *will* be married in a chapel."

"No, I will not!" Laura replied emphatically.

The psychic's voice suddenly became firm and direct. Her voice rose, and she forcefully said to Laura, "Jesus was a good man, but he is not the son of God!" Her outburst against Jesus continued for what seemed like another ten minutes. Laura listened carefully for the full ten minutes. Then she had heard enough.

Laura interrupted her. "Lady, why are you preaching at me? I'm not a Christian. I don't believe in Christ! I paid you ten dollars to tell my future. I want you to tell my future, not preach at me!"

"You don't belong here!" The psychic's voice rose again. "You don't belong here!" Then she became very quiet. In a few moments, she spoke again. "Your spirit guide told me many things about you. I know you are planning to move to California, but you should not go. But nobody can tell you anything. You are just as stubborn as your father! And you *are* getting married in a chapel."

"But why shouldn't I go to California?"

"You will have a very hard time if you go to California. You should not move. If you go, by the end of this year, you will die!" Then she went on to predict in great detail what Laura's life would be like for the next twenty-two years. She foretold years of family discord, problems in a future marriage, and serious health difficulties. But after all of these things happened, she predicted, Laura would enjoy great happiness and success.

It was a very upsetting experience because the forecast for the next twenty-two years, predicted in great detail, included many painful events. Everything this psychic had predicted in the past had come true, down to each minute detail. Laura regretted seeing her and wished she had never gone.

What did the psychic mean when she said that Laura would die? If she predicted the next twenty-two years, it was obvious it was not a physical death. So what kind of death would it be? The psychic was correct that Laura's father was stubborn. She was correct about another family member's life choices. She was correct about Laura moving to California. That was her plan, and no one could stop her. Now she was predicting that Laura would marry an auburn-haired man in a Protestant wedding. As Laura saw it, she was predicting that Laura would become a Protestant and be disowned by her family.

Gathering up her things, Laura hastily left the psychic's house; this time she felt chilled right down to her toes. She never returned. A deep fear of the supernatural began to settle into Laura's mind—a very deep fear. This psychic was like nothing Laura had ever known, but somehow, the fear was similar to what she had felt with the Ouija board when she was nine years old. She decided to have nothing to do with the supernatural or psychics ever again.

All the next day Laura considered what the psychic had said. She had every intention of moving to California, but she couldn't ignore the negative predictions of what might happen if she went. Laura was feeling edgy and ill at ease when she went to bed that night. She tossed and turned and finally fell into a restless sleep. Then she had a dream that she remembered vividly the next morning. It was like no dream she had ever had—as if she were experiencing it while awake, in vivid color, and not as a dream.

She was back on the farm, running through the fields, as she had so often done for fun as a child. Back and forth she ran, feeling happy and enjoying the wind blowing through her hair. She put out her arms as children do, and suddenly, she was lifting off the ground, flying through the air. She flew higher and higher, looking down at the house, the barns, and the familiar outbuildings. She could see the cows in the field, the pigs and the chickens, and her brothers and sisters moving about, doing their farm chores. She flew higher and higher; the buildings grew smaller; and now she could see all of the fields that surrounded the farm. Flying filled her with great joy and a sense of freedom.

Higher still she flew. Then, to her surprise, she saw that a massive stone wall completely surrounded the farm. The wall was built of huge dark-red stones, cemented together to form an impenetrable barrier. Laura guessed that it was about twenty feet high and ten feet wide and appeared to have no gates and no way out. She flew all around it, looking for an opening, but there was none. The wall was solid. It was a prison wall! Her family was locked inside a prison with no way out! She had to tell them.

In her dream, she flew back to earth and gathered all ten of her brothers and sisters together. "We're in a prison! There's a huge wall around the farm, and there is no gate and no way out! The only way to escape is to fly up and over the wall."

Her siblings looked at her in utter disbelief. "You're crazy, Laura! There's no wall. We've lived here our entire lives, and we've never seen a wall. And besides, you can't fly. We don't believe what you're saying."

"I _can_ fly! Watch me!" Laura put out her arms and once again, lifted off the ground. But most of her siblings wouldn't even look. They just shook their heads, turned their backs on her, and walked away.

But Bill and Lois stayed. "Teach us how to fly," Bill said.

"Yeah, Laura, we want to know how," Lois added.

Laura was relieved that at least two of her siblings believed her. "OK," she said happily, "I'll teach you." And she put out her arms once again and showed them what to do, hovering just above their heads.

At that point in her dream, things turned ugly. Her mother looked out the kitchen window and saw what they were doing. She stormed out of the house with a broom in her hand, yelling at the top of her lungs.

"Laura Sicking, come down here right now!" she shrieked. "What do you think you are doing? Don't you know flying is evil? No one should fly! It is a wicked, sinful thing to do!" She tried to beat at Laura with the broom handle, but Laura flew upwards. Her mother continued to rant and rave, swiping ineffectively at her daughter who hovered above the ground, just out of her reach. Finally, her mother gave up and, still raving, stomped back into the house.

When she was gone, Lois and Bill entreated Laura again. "Please, please teach us how to fly," they begged. Laura started with Lois. Her sister, who was five feet nine inches tall, weighed about three hundred pounds. Again and again Laura demonstrated how to fly, and Lois tried her best to do exactly as she was shown, but she couldn't get off the ground.

"Lois, you're just too heavy. I think you're going to have to change the way you live before you will be able to fly."

Lois shrugged. "Well, forget that," she said. "If I have to make any lifestyle changes, then I guess I'm never going to fly." She turned and walked away.

Next Laura showed Bill how to fly, but before they got far, her mother, who saw her teaching Lois and Bill, tried again to beat her with the broom handle. Laura flew upwards, hovering there, waiting until their mother once again gave up and left.

Bill was having trouble too. Although he wasn't fat, he was a big guy, nearly six and a half feet tall. He struggled and struggled to get off the ground. "Bill, let me try holding you with one arm, and I'll use the other arm to give you a lift." They tried again, but even with Laura's help, Bill just couldn't take off.

"I can't do it, Laura! I just can't get the hang of it!" Bill was frustrated.

"Well, Bill," Laura said in her dream, "I can't do it for you. You have to choose to fly, and do it entirely by yourself."

Once again their mother intervened, broom in hand, screeching that flying was evil and demanding that Laura come down.

Just then, Laura heard a voice in her dream: *"Fly away! Leave the prison. Go to the west. Go to California."* And Laura did, soaring higher and higher until the farm, the prison wall, the town of Muenster, and the whole state of Texas disappeared.

When Laura awoke, she laid quietly in her bed, reliving and contemplating the dream. It was a strange, puzzling dream. Laura loved her mother and wanted to view her with the utmost respect and in the most positive of terms, but the dream did not show her that way. The dream portrayed Laura as the only one leaving the family, with most of her siblings walking away from her, and her mother angry about Laura's decision to fly and even condemning it as evil. Her father wasn't in the dream at all. Why was that? Then there was the voice, encouraging Laura to fly west to California—the exact opposite of what the psychic said she should do. Was the dream warning her of what her future relationship with her mother and her siblings would be like?

It would be another seven months before the significance of this dream would become clear to Laura. She came to believe that the dream was God's way of saying, *"Brace yourself, Laura. You're heading into some major headwinds. Things are going to be hard. These events must happen. But I will give you a way to escape."* The memory of that dream gave Laura great solace through the decades of family discord that were soon to follow. Although she didn't know it yet, God would continue to use dreams to guide and comfort her.

CHAPTER 15

....

"I Quit Drinking Yesterday"

May 5, 1981, was graduation day! The big auditorium at Texas Tech was filled with jubilant black-gowned graduates, and Laura was among them. It was a great day. Her mother and her sister Lois made the trip from Muenster, and they were in the audience when Laura received her diploma. She was now a college graduate with a bachelor of science degree in chemical engineering. Laura had just completed a major step in her long-range plan to become the happy, successful person she wanted to be and to gain her family's respect and love.

Laura was happy to have two members of her family witness her graduation. She didn't expect her father to come. He never went to anything, but having her mom and Lois at the ceremony pleased her immensely.

Her family was far flung by this time. Most of the siblings would eventually become high achievers, making successful careers for themselves and marrying successful spouses. Virginia had married Hank, and they had both finished college. Virginia, always talented and creative, had earned a bachelor's degree in fashion merchandising and design and a master's in business administration. Hank had a master's degree in engineering and would go on to earn his doctorate in the field of international relations. Hank worked for Otis Engineering, a subsidiary of the Halliburton Company. The pair was living in London, where Hank supervised regional oil drilling operations for the company.

Deb became a nurse anesthetist. Julie became a medical technologist and an accountant. Brian owned a successful car repair and body shop, and Bill became a nurse. Mark became a mechanic with his own diesel repair shop. Over time, he would find adult life overwhelming and each new day a difficult challenge.

Joyce invited Laura to take a trip with her to visit Hank and Virginia in London after graduation. Joyce's husband, Paul, was unable to take time off from his busy practice for the monthlong trip, and Joyce didn't want to go alone. She and Paul could easily afford the trip, but Laura, fresh out of college and weighed down by student loans, could not. "No problem," said Joyce. "I'll lend you the money, and when you get your first couple of paychecks, you can pay me back."

Immediately after graduation, Laura shipped her few worldly goods to California and flew west to meet Joyce. She was so excited to be leaving Texas that she could hardly breathe during the whole trip. To help calm herself down, she wrote a long letter to Tom, telling him about the graduation ceremony and her plans for the future. Then she wrote another letter to herself, congratulating herself on her accomplishments.

The plane touched down on California soil, and Joyce was there to meet her. The two of them flew on to London. They spent two weeks in the city with Virginia and Hank and the rest of their time on a guided bus tour of European countries. The sisters enjoyed the trip and grew closer than ever. Both still suffered from their addictions: Joyce from her eating disorder, and Laura with her alcoholism. Neither discussed her problems with the other, but they had a good time together.

The tour guide told everyone on the bus that it was not safe to drink the tap water because of widespread parasite contamination and strongly suggested buying bottled water. Laura had a real problem with the idea of paying for water, especially when she noticed that it cost about the same as beer. *If I'm going to pay for it anyway, I might as well drink beer*, she thought. After the first day, however, she realized that she couldn't function while drinking beer all day long, and she resorted to buying water like the other tourists.

On her return from Europe, Laura went directly to Bakersfield, California, where her first job awaited her. Her possessions arrived, and she was soon comfortably set up in a two-bedroom apartment in a decent area on a busy road, within easy biking distance of her new office. She had a little money, and she used it to furnish her apartment with garage-sale finds. She didn't mind living frugally. She was used to it. She planned to work hard, save her money, pay off her school debts, and go to medical school.

It was delightful to have a place of her own. At home, she had lived in a dormlike room with several of her sisters. At college, she had usually had a roommate, although, after a couple of unfortunate experiences, she had demanded and gotten a small dorm room to herself. Having all of this space to call her own was a new experience. She offered Melissa, her good friend from college, a place to stay if she didn't find a job right away. But so far, Melissa hadn't taken her up on the offer, and Laura was happy to live alone.

The major thing that marred her new life was her dependence on alcohol. Although she was managing to show the world an accomplished, competent young woman, she couldn't go twenty-four hours without a drink. She was afraid the problem was getting worse. She was determined that it wouldn't interfere with her new life and her new job.

Laura was glad to have a job waiting for her. She had attended a job fair at Texas Tech, where various companies sent representatives to interview graduating students. She signed up for interviews with quite a few of the companies. All but two of the companies were located in Texas. One of the two was the Getty Oil Company's refinery in Bakersfield, California. They offered her a job.

Laura looked at Bakersfield on a map of the state. It was located about two hours' drive from Los Angeles and two and a half hours' drive from the beach. The mountains were close, and it was only a four- or five-hour drive to Las Vegas! Laura, who played poker and blackjack with her siblings, liked the idea of being so close to the gambling capital of the world.

California was paradise! That was all she needed to know. She could spend her weekends at the beach! It was perfect, and she snapped up the job.

Her first day at Getty Oil was June 29, 1981. She arrived on her bike, found her office, and began to settle in. Introductions were made, and one of the first people she met was a tall young man named Mike. Mike was an engineering student at the University of California in Santa Barbara, serving a summer internship at Getty Oil. Laura, brand new on the job, would be overseeing his work.

The attraction between the two young people was immediate. It wasn't long before they got to know each other quite well. Mike was about five feet ten inches tall and very, very thin—so thin he looked undernourished. His eyes were deep set in his angular face, and his dark, straight hair fell over a high forehead.

After they knew each other for a few weeks, Mike invited her to dinner at a Mexican restaurant. It was their first date, and they had a great time. Then she invited him over to her apartment and cooked him dinner. The meal wasn't terribly successful. Mike was a die-hard vegetarian, and Laura hadn't yet learned to cook vegetarian meals well. But she was still very much against eating white sugar, and they talked about that and shared their ideas about health and diet.

As the evening progressed, they began to talk about religion—a subject that Laura always found fascinating. Mike told her he was a Seventh-day Adventist and had been one for about two years.

"A Seventh-day Adventist? Is that a Christian religion?"

Mike nodded.

"I wonder why I've never encountered that one before," Laura said. She told Mike about her search to find a Christian religion with doctrines that she could believe in and how she had visited every Protestant church in the phone book; three different phone books, in fact. How could she have missed the

Seventh-day Adventist Church? "Well, tell me about Seventh-day Adventists, Mike. What do you believe?"

Mike told her that Seventh-day Adventists believe that Jesus is the Son of God, that He is coming to earth again soon, and that Adventists keep the seventh day of the week, Saturday, as the Sabbath. Laura listened avidly; her mind, as always, was eager to learn something new.

She asked him more about the vegetarian thing, and he told her a little about the Adventist emphasis on a healthy lifestyle. They got into some of the doctrines of his church, except, for some reason, the church's position on the state of the dead and hell. She was interested in it all from a purely philosophical point of view.

Mike invited her to go to church with him. "Sure!" she replied. "I would like that. No point in leaving the Seventh-day Adventists off my list!"

So she went with him to church. Noticing the book rack as they entered the building, Laura's sharp eye spotted a copy of *Steps to Christ*. She thought idly, *I wonder why they have a Baptist book here?* The sermon that day was about what happens to people when they die. She learned that Seventh-day Adventists believe the Bible teaches that death is a state of unconscious sleep until Jesus' second coming and the resurrection. There was no going to heaven when a person died and, more important to Laura, no eternally burning hell.

That makes sense! she thought. That idea of an eternally burning hell was the sticking point that had kept her from returning to any of the Protestant churches she had visited. Most preached some version of that. She was so turned off by it that she decided that reincarnation made more sense. Listening to this Adventist preacher, she thought, *This makes more sense than reincarnation!* Her heart was also touched. *I can believe this*, she thought. *This is consistent with what I know about God. I like this sermon.* She attended church with Mike the next Sabbath and the next. They continued to go to church together every Sabbath that whole summer.

When Mike and Laura had been dating for a few months, she began to wonder what the future of their relationship would be. As she often did when thinking about the future, she picked up a deck of playing cards and, using them as tarot cards, laid them out to read her fortune. Although she made up her mind never to see a psychic again after her painful and frightening experience in Lubbock, she made no connection between the psychic and telling her own fortune with the playing cards. Reading the cards was just a game.

As she had done many times before, she sat at her kitchen table, shuffled the fifty-two cards, and dealt them into four piles. Each pile of cards stood for the major categories of life, including a person's love life or marriage, financial state or career, and health. The numbers on the cards stood for good or bad outcomes in these areas. When she finished dealing, she was stunned to see that all four piles showed the worst possible conclusions in all areas of her life—the worst predictions of pain, loneliness, financial problems, and misery she could possibly imagine!

Laura was shocked and frightened. This was far too similar to the psychic's predictions. She shuffled the cards again and dealt them into four piles, and once again they revealed the exact same dreadful outcomes in all areas of her life. Laura knew that statistically it was virtually impossible for the cards to come up exactly the same way twice. But they had. Suddenly, she felt uneasy about even touching the cards. It was similar to the feeling she had years ago when she and her siblings had experimented with the Ouija board. She tossed the cards aside and tried to put the whole episode out of her mind. However, the next time she saw Mike she told him what happened.

"Laura, those cards are connecting you to the occult. They're the same as going to a psychic. I believe that stuff is dangerous and evil. The devil is in it." Mike told her about a book he had purchased recently in an Adventist bookstore. It dealt with all aspects of the supernatural and the occult and the dangers inherent in them.

Mike loaned Laura the book. She read it from cover to cover and immediately threw away everything in her house that had to do with psychics, séances, black magic, fortune-telling, and tarot cards. She got rid of her books and all the cards she could find, throwing away about eight different sets of cards. From that day forward, she never allowed another deck of playing cards in her house.

Then Mike gave her a King James Bible. In high school, when she was traveling with the track team, she had stolen a Gideon Bible from a motel, not knowing that these Bibles were put there to be taken by anybody who wanted them. She discovered it in the drawer of the bedside table, and lacking anything else to read, tried to read it in a few days. She didn't get far and couldn't comprehend much. In a last-ditch effort to understand, she jumped to Psalms and Proverbs, and something changed. She found those verses poetic, and she was a lover of poetry.

I've got to have this book, she thought and into her suitcase it went. Her teammates saw it in her luggage and thought it was funny. "Laura stole a Bible!" they chanted, pointing fingers at her. She pretended not to care, but she felt so guilty about her theft that she didn't touch the Bible for several years. When things got tough in college, however, she rediscovered those beautiful poems, and they brought her solace and comfort. But that was as far as she had gotten.

Now she decided she needed to read this book from cover to cover. She couldn't imagine why she never had. Laura read many books, but the Bible was different. She found it so foreign and the language so difficult to understand that she couldn't just zip through it. However, she started with the first chapter in Genesis and slowly began to read it through. When she got to the New Testament, she found the Book a little easier to read, and soon she was zipping through it in her usual way.

In the back of her mind was the old familiar craving for a drink, and she was doing her best to ignore it, but it was growing stronger. Then she got to a text that stopped her cold. It was in the book of John, chapter 16, verses 23 and 24. Jesus was talking to the disciples, and He said to them, "Very truly I tell you, my Father will give you whatever you ask in my name. Until now you have not asked for anything in my name. Ask and you will receive, and your joy will be complete."

Laura looked up from the Bible. *Really?* she thought. *Is it really possible that this Jesus meant this for everybody, even for somebody like me? I can't go twenty-four hours without a drink, and I am really craving alcohol right now. If I asked . . .*

Right then and there she bowed her head and said this prayer: "God, if this Bible is Your Word and if Jesus is Your Son and if You really care about us down here, please get rid of the alcohol in my life. I'm craving it right now, and I want it badly. I'm trying with all my strength not to drink, but I can't stop on my own. I have no strength against this bad habit. I'm desperate, and I need help. In Jesus' name, amen."

The craving for alcohol that she was fighting just seconds before was instantly gone! It was just gone! *Wow! This is amazing! Now this is power*, Laura thought. She sat quietly, enjoying the experience of not feeling the craving that had been her constant companion for years. *Let's see if I make it for twenty-four hours*, she told herself. *That is my uppermost limit.*

Twenty-four hours later, there was still no craving for alcohol, but she was ravenous. She was tempted to eat compulsively. So she went back to God with this prayer, "OK, God, You did great on bad habit number one. Let's move on to bad habit number two. I'm craving food when I'm not even hungry. I can't stop; I'm desperate, and I need help. I can't do it on my own. Will You please get rid of this craving too?"

The craving to eat compulsively was gone immediately. *Wow! This is amazing! Now this is power!* Skeptical, Laura thought once again, *OK, let's see if I can make it for twenty-four hours.* And twenty-four hours later, both cravings were still gone. They never returned. She praised God for giving her the victory over both alcohol and compulsive eating. What wonderful freedom!

Laura talked to God again. "OK, God," she prayed. "You did great on bad habits number one and number two. I have about fifty more bad habits. Let me bring them all out right here. Let's clean house. Let's get rid of them all." From that moment on, Laura felt the power to begin to make the changes her life required, although many of these changes would take years to accomplish. God was with her.

As her new walk with the Lord developed, that power to make changes became the thing she appreciated most about her growing relationship with God. He gave her the power to overcome her bad habits. He could stop her from sabotaging and destroying her own life.

She had a dinner date with Mike the next evening. Laura ordered first, and then Mike told their server what he wanted, including his wine selection.

"Did you forget to order wine, Laura?"

Mike was a social drinker. He assumed she was too. Laura had hid her dependency on alcohol from him. They both usually ordered wine with their meals, and she served him drinks at home. "You know what, Mike," she said quietly. "I quit drinking yesterday."

"You quit drinking? What do you mean?" replied Mike. She told him the whole story of her longtime dependency on alcohol and how the Lord gave her the victory over it.

Mike was happy for her and decided that if she wasn't drinking he wouldn't either. He canceled his order.

Mike hadn't mentioned to Laura that Adventists abstain from drinking alcohol. She wouldn't find that out for several months. They discussed diet and agreed that neither would eat meat because he was very much opposed to it, and it was at this point that Laura finally became a full-time vegetarian. Nor would they eat sugary desserts—something she was adamant about. But, up to that point, alcohol had never come up.

CHAPTER 16

....

"We're Going to Have to Cut You Out of There"

L aura, how about following me down to Santa Barbara in your car when I go back to school?" Mike's question was no surprise. His only mode of transportation was a motorcycle, and he had a lot of stuff. Laura agreed to trail him in the Vega, which they would load with his clothes and other possessions.

She couldn't believe her first summer in California was nearly over. It was a great summer. For the first time in many years, she was free of her alcohol dependency. Not only that, but her job was going well, and she and Mike enjoyed their free time together, including frequent trips to the beach. California was definitely living up to her expectations. She was living the life of her dreams.

The journey to Santa Barbara was a three-hour trip over major California freeways, and in no time, they arrived at Mike's dorm on the campus of the university. Laura helped him unload his things from the Vega, they said their farewells, and soon she was back on the road to go home. She decided to take the "shortcut" through the mountains. It was a beautiful clear, sunny day, and she intended to enjoy the drive home through some beautiful California mountain scenery.

So, about twelve miles east of Santa Barbara, she left the main road to take the Maricopa Highway through the Los Padres National Forest. The road soon changed from gentle curves to torturous mountain switchbacks; each one was tighter than the last. Laura slowed her car, but it took all of her concentration to hold the Vega on the road through the hairpin curves. There was only one lane going each way, and the road's shoulder was extremely narrow. It was almost nonexistent in some places. She passed through Ojai—a pretty town that is famous for its natural beauty and charming Spanish-style architecture—and still the road climbed.

She reached a place where the switchbacks were longer, which gave her an opportunity to see other cars coming toward her. On one side of the road, the mountain rose steeply, and on the other, it dropped off precipitously, with only a low metal guardrail for safety. The traffic wasn't heavy, but there was an occasional vehicle coming slowly down the mountainside as she continued to drive up, going about twenty miles an hour.

She heard the sound of a loud engine and looked up to see a dark-colored Jeep coming toward her, going much too fast. *What's the matter with that guy?* she thought while applying her brakes. What occurred next happened so fast that it was only afterward that she was able to reconstruct it. The Jeep, unable to make the curve, hit the guardrail at more than fifty miles an hour, bounced off it, crossed the road, and shot up the side of the mountain. It rolled over and then bounced back down to the road, just as Laura and her little brown Vega arrived at that very spot. It landed on top of her car, stopped it cold, flattened it, and pinned her inside it. The Jeep then ended right-side up against the guardrail on the other side of the road.

Laura was unable to move. There was glass everywhere, and she was covered with blood from a multitude of cuts. Blood and glass were in her eyes and in her mouth. One arm was hanging uselessly at her side. Her seat belt held her in place, but the roof of the Vega was flattened so low that she couldn't raise her head. But, amazingly, she was conscious.

To her astonishment, the driver of the Jeep climbed out of his car, ambled over to her, leaned down, and peered in the shattered window. "Man, am I glad you were there!" He pushed his long blond hair out of his eyes and grinned at her. "If you hadn't stopped my car, I would have gone right over that guardrail and down the mountain! If you hadn't been there, I would have died!"

Is he high? she thought. He was obviously under the influence of something. By this time, other cars had stopped, and Laura heard a siren in the distance. Soon a California Highway Patrol officer appeared and took charge of the situation. "How are you doing?" he asked. "Are you OK?"

Laura nodded weakly. "I'm cut up pretty bad, and my arm is hurting. I think it's broken. And I can't move."

The cop leaned in, took a good look at her, and said, "Looks like you had your seat belt on."

"Yes, I did," Laura replied.

"That's why you're alive. Without it, you would have gone right through that windshield," he said, gesturing at the gaping hole where her windshield had been. "We're going to have to cut you out of there," he added.

He called for backup with the necessary equipment. Once it arrived it took several hours to cut and pry the wreck apart and free Laura. As she was being lifted onto a stretcher, she caught a glimpse of her car. It was only three or four feet high! She couldn't believe she survived that wreck. They put her in an ambulance, placing on top of her a plastic bag containing the contents of her glove box, including the little book *Steps to Christ*. She was taken to the hospital back in Ojai.

Laura's injuries appeared to be remarkably light considering the nature of the accident. She had a broken arm and various cuts and bruises. The worst consequence wasn't as apparent, however. Her seat belt may well have saved her life; but by holding her in place, it caused the ligaments in her hips to be so stretched that she would never be able to run long distances or ski again, despite many years of physical therapy.

After only a few hours at the hospital, Laura was back in her apartment. As she struggled to prepare a meal for herself, she was filled with despair. Her right arm was in a cast. She hurt all over. She had no car. She couldn't ride her bike to work. It was going to be a struggle to even take care of herself. She felt very much alone. How was she going to manage? It was barely dark when she took one of the pills for pain she had been given at the hospital and went to bed.

She lay in bed for hours that night and waited for sleep to come. But each time she closed her eyes, she saw that dark-colored Jeep coming toward her at a terrifying speed. *That was my third brush with death*, she thought. *First, the suicide thing, then the kidney failure, and now this.* Each time her life was miraculously saved. In the light of her renewed relationship with a loving, powerful, and benevolent God, she was beginning to see a pattern, and she was profoundly thankful. Once again she was given another chance.

She lay awake, and she began to ponder her whole approach to life in light of what had just happened. She thought back over her past. When she was fourteen and planned her own death, she revised her thinking about herself. She resolved then to free herself from being victimized. Instead, she planned to lead a successful life. She was determined to make herself happy and show her family that she was worthy and lovable. She became pretty good at it, achieving her goals to educate herself and to land a job that commanded her family's respect.

Then this accident happened. One of her first thoughts was, *What if I had died?* And something dawned on her. She wouldn't have died contented. The success she achieved hadn't made her happy. Most of what she had accomplished thus far in life was done to please her family. She wasn't free at all. She still cared desperately about what they thought of her. *If I had died tonight*, she thought, *I would not have lived the life I wanted to live. I would not have lived for myself.*

She did everything within her power to create the person she thought her family wanted her to be. But there were many things that had become a part of her since she went to college, especially in the last few months—things that must be hidden from them. There were things she knew would offend them, such as becoming a vegetarian, her search for a religion to replace Catholicism in her life, reading the Bible, gaining victory over alcohol, and even her whole worldview of the importance of truth.

She was so desperately afraid of displeasing her mother and of never being able to win her love that instead of finding joy in her own growth as a person, she continued to live a secret life, which her family could never know about. But what kind of a way to live was that? She wanted deeper, more open relationships in her life. She wanted to be herself.

She realized that many of the things she wanted out of life were the direct opposite of her family's expectations. She needed to live her own life and be her own person, even if her decisions meant that she might never see her family again. At this thought, she felt herself grow cold with dread. The very thought of not having her family's respect and love still filled her, as it always had, with anxiety.

Nope, she thought, *I have to be strong. Anxiety cannot control my life. From now on, I'm living my life for myself. And if they don't like it, that's their problem. They can take me or leave me. I am not going to be held captive to the need to please them anymore. If I die tomorrow, I want to be happy with how I live today. Maybe the car wreck had to happen to help me understand that.*

It might seem crazy to be thankful for a car wreck, but in a way, she was glad it happened. She had an important new insight that would play a significant role in all of her future decisions. She breathed one more prayer of thanksgiving for her life and drifted off to sleep with one thought in her mind: *If I die tomorrow, I want to be happy with how I live today.*

This became her motto for life.

The next morning Laura awoke with a start. Sunshine was streaming in her bedroom window, and the doorbell was ringing insistently. She struggled out of bed, into a robe, and opened her apartment door. There stood Melissa, her old friend from Texas Tech, with a suitcase in each hand.

"What happened to you?" Melissa's face showed the shock she felt at seeing Laura in her banged-up condition. Laura was really glad to see her. She put her one good arm around her friend, invited her in, and told her the whole story.

"You said I could come," Melissa said, "and here I am. Looks like I got here just in time!" Melissa had not found a job and was determined not to go back home to live with her family. For the next several months, she took tender care of Laura, driving her to work every day, cooking her meals, and nursing her back to health and strength. Laura's heart was filled with gratitude for the kindness God showed her by sending Melissa just when she needed her the most.

CHAPTER 17

....

"Well, You Need to Read This Book"

As Laura slowly healed from her injuries, she continued her plan to read the Bible through. When she came to a text in Matthew 5:44, 45, in which Jesus said, "Love your enemies and pray for those who persecute you, that you may be children of your Father in heaven," that stopped her cold. She immediately thought of her father and how she hated him. It was impossible for her to love him with things as they were.

"God, You know how much I hate him," she began to pray. "You know I would have mowed him down with a machine gun if I could have—and You know why. I would have killed him any way I could have. The only thing that stopped me was the fear of prison.

"If You really mean it about loving your enemies, if You want me to love him, God, You are going to have to change my heart. I'm not able to love him. He doesn't deserve my love."

During the next few days, she prayed this prayer over and over as she pondered this text and the impossibility of loving her father. Then questions began to form in her mind; questions she had never thought about before: *What kind of family did he have? What kind of life did he grow up with? What was his father like? His mother?*

If Laura's four years of therapy while in college taught her anything, it was that people lived to repeat what they grew up with unless they learned otherwise. Her father never had therapy. Did he grow up in an abusive home? She tried to remember what bits and pieces she had heard over the years.

Her father never talked about his childhood. Her mother knew nothing about it. But she knew that his parents' marriage was an arranged one. His mother had been thirteen or fourteen at the time, and the man she married had been thirty-five. From what little Laura heard, she assumed that the marriage was an unhappy one, maybe even an abusive one. It was quite possible her father was raised in an abusive home. That wouldn't excuse what he did, but perhaps God was leading her to feel some compassion for him.

Over the next few months, Laura made inquiries, talking with some of her sisters and others in the family. Her sisters had no definite information about his childhood, but the family stories raised some red flags. Laura herself remembered a family get-together when she was about twelve. Her dad had been about forty years old then. He was standing around talking with several of his brothers when something was said, and an all-out fistfight erupted. There were no signs of an argument, just a sudden change from conversation to grown men rolling around on the ground, beating each other up.

Her sisters recalled hearing the story of Grandmother Sicking, her dad's mother. When Grandpa Sicking died, she stood up at the lunch after the funeral and made a statement: "If you think I'm sad this man is dead, you're crazy. I'm going to live the rest of my life for myself." That didn't sound as though they had a healthy relationship.

Another family story was even more telling. When Grandma was eight months pregnant with her sixth child, Emmett, she had pneumonia. She was not allowed to receive treatment for her illness, and her husband forced her to work in the fields, as their German culture expected. Somehow both she and the baby survived, although the baby was born with pneumonia. After she recovered from both pneumonia and the birth, Grandma decided that she would no longer work in the fields, and she never did again. For the next twenty-five years, she pretended to be sick in bed whenever her husband was around.

Then there was the story that during their marriage she had left her husband and gone to live with her in-laws for three years. Laura wondered what that was about.

Laura's father had several brothers, and Laura considered what she knew of their families. There was a great deal of dysfunction there. One uncle married and had two sons, but the family life became so bad that his wife divorced him and left with their sons. The sons changed their names and refused to see or talk to their father again for the rest of their lives. All of these stories convinced her that her father had a difficult childhood and that there was a strong probability he may have been abused—sexually, verbally, physically, or all three. No doubt he, too, felt rejected, abandoned, and unloved. Although she would never know for certain, she reasoned he may have also been a victim—a helpless child, too weak to prevent being abused.

With God's miraculous help, she began the slow and difficult work of forgiving her father in her heart. During the next few years, God continued to help her overcome her anger and to find a level of compassion for the man who gave her life. "I've hurt other people, I know, God. Please forgive me and give me the strength to forgive those who have hurt me."

Laura still had a great deal of work to do before she could completely come to terms with the childhood abuse she endured or bring herself to speak to her father about it. For now, it was enough that God put the first seeds of forgiveness toward him in her heart, and she was grateful for the power that God's grace gave her to change.

Laura continued to read the Bible. She read it all the way through several times from Genesis to the end of Revelation. She developed a genuine respect for God's Word, but she felt that she didn't understand the Bible. She found it to be a complex Book. Despite her reading, she still had two big questions for which she needed answers: What is truth? And why didn't God answer her prayers for help as a little girl?

Mike suggested that she get a concordance so she could study the Bible topically and search out what it said about various subjects. Laura, who had never heard of a concordance, thought that was a terrific idea. So she bought a *Strong's Concordance* and began to look up every reference to truth in the Bible. She found that there were several definitions of truth in the Bible, and she really liked them all. She read that God's Word is truth, God's commandments are truth, the sum of God's Word is truth, the law is truth, and God's works are truth.

She especially liked that last one: God's works are truth. She assumed that meant the world of nature. From her years of studying science, she knew that the universe obeys certain natural laws and that they never change. No matter what humans do, those universal laws of nature remain the same. She was always drawn to nature, partly for just that reason, and found great solace in it. God's works are truth. Yes, she could buy that. That passed her litmus test.

Then she read John 14:6, "I am the way and the truth and the life. No one comes to the Father except through me." Jesus said this to His disciples. That connected with her too. Jesus is truth. Studying the Bible in this way was a new and wonderful experience.

Yet, it was a sad situation that she searched for truth her entire life, working her way systematically through the writings and doctrines of every religion and church in existence, without ever finding the simple, beautiful truth that this Book contained. Did she really have to get to the point where she threw out everything she was taught as a Catholic and eliminate every known religion before she was ready to understand the truth from the Bible?

She thought back to her first week in Bakersfield. One of the first things she did after getting settled in her apartment was to go through the Yellow Pages to see if there were any churches listed that she hadn't tried yet. She was looking for anything, even branches of denominations she had already visited. She came across one group called the Missouri Synod of the Lutheran Church.

I don't think I've ever visited them, she thought. So, on her first Sunday in Bakersfield, she found the church and took her place in a pew. The message from the pulpit that day was clear: if you weren't a member of the Missouri Synod of the Lutheran Church, you were lost.

Oh, I am so sick of this! I heard that doctrine in the Catholic Church and in so many churches since then. I reject that. It is completely false. No religion can claim to have a corner on the market! For the first time in all the years she spent visiting churches, Laura got up and walked out in the middle of the sermon.

She went home that day and thought about her situation. She felt that she had exhausted the various paths to find truth and still hadn't found it. Where was she to go now? She didn't know. For the first time in ten years, she decided to pray. "God," she prayed, "I am so sick and tired of all the churches I have attended. I don't agree with any of them! I hope You understand, but I am not going to go to another church—not to any service at all—until You let me know where to go. I'm giving up. I'm finished."

The very next week she went to the Seventh-day Adventist church with Mike because he asked her, because he was cute and she liked him, and because one more church couldn't hurt. Was that also a part of God's plan?

Now she was beginning to understand what truth was. She was attending church regularly with Mike and liking what she heard there. She was enjoying the Bible, liking what she found there, and agreeing with it. But she wanted more.

"Why don't you go to the Adventist bookstore and see if you can find some books that look interesting?" Mike suggested. "There's a store right here in Bakersfield, not far from where we work."

That was all Laura needed to hear. When she entered the little bookstore for the first time, she walked around slowly, picking up first one book and then another. She was deeply engrossed in reading the back cover of a particular book when the salesclerk asked, "Are you looking for anything in particular?"

Laura turned and met Verna Hamilton, who was about Laura's height, slender, with bright eyes and blond, curly hair. Her smile was warm, and her manner was outgoing and friendly.

Laura felt comfortable with Verna right away. "Well, I'm dating a guy who's an Adventist, and I'm going to church with him. I want to know more about what Adventists believe. I'm looking for some books that explain Adventist beliefs."

"Oh," said Verna, "which church are you and your boyfriend attending?"

"It's called Bakersfield Central. My boyfriend is in college in Santa Barbara; but he comes back to Bakersfield every weekend, and we go to church together."

"Oh, well, that explains why I haven't seen you at church. My family and I attend

Hillcrest. So you want to learn something more about what Adventists believe?"

"I do."

"Well, you may enjoy reading this book on Adventist doctrines," said Verna, picking a thick volume off the shelf. "This book on Bible prophecy and this book on the life of Christ are quite interesting too," she said. Her eyes sparkled as she went from table to table, adding books on various topics to the growing pile in Laura's arms. "Are those too many?" she asked.

"Let me look at all of them. I read a lot, and I think I would enjoy them!" said Laura, and she bought most of them.

Laura and Verna became close friends. Laura learned more about Adventists' interest in healthy living and in particular about Verna's eating habits. She didn't eat white sugar either; in fact, she was very strict about her diet. *Wow!* thought Laura. *I've found somebody who thinks like I do!* Verna was always sweet and thoughtful and handled Laura's questions with tact.

CHAPTER 18

"How Precious Did That Grace Appear"

One day Laura noticed an announcement for a series of meetings being presented in the Bakersfield Civic Auditorium, which were sponsored by Seventh-day Adventists. It was going to be a long series—five nights a week for about eight weeks. Laura and Melissa decided to go, but they missed the first couple of weeks. By the time they began attending, evangelist Dick Pollard was deep into discussing world history in light of Bible prophecy. They attended most of the rest of the series, slipping into the huge auditorium each night and taking seats in the back. They were just two anonymous young women among the thousand or so people who attended.

Dick Pollard carefully presented Bible prophecy and showed how each prophecy was fulfilled in history. Laura listened intently. One night he presented the prophecies in the second chapter of the book of Daniel that, he explained, predicted the rise and fall of four major world empires, spanning two thousand years. Laura was amazed as she listened to these Bible prophecies that were written hundreds of years before the events they described occurred. *That's it!* she thought. *That's the objective answer I've been looking for—the answer I need to prove that the Bible is the truth. History proves that the Bible's prophecies are true. This proves that I can believe in the Bible.*

Then Pollard began to speak about the shocking history of the Catholic Church: the Inquisition, the selling of indulgences, the torture and execution of Protestant Reformers, the suppression of the Bible, other things that the church did, and how these things were predicted in biblical prophecies. Laura was blown away. Of course, she was aware of some of the darker aspects of Catholicism's history, but she never heard before that the church was linked to Bible prophecy.

She was astounded and shocked. She bought more books at the Adventist bookstore and read more deeply into the history of Catholicism as it is linked to Bible prophecy. *How could anybody have the guts to say these things in public or write them in a book?* It was amazing to her that the Bible condemned the Catholic Church's shameful history and practices and predicted that they would happen. For Laura, this explained why the Catholic Church had suppressed the Bible for centuries.

I've got to study this stuff in the Bible, she thought. *I have to study it in detail. I know this history of the Catholic Church is true*, she thought. *I've lived some of it. I know how evil and destructive some of those strict Catholic doctrines can be. I've seen them destroy lives. They very nearly destroyed mine. These Adventists believe the way I do.*

Later it would cross her mind as odd that her thought was, *They believe the way I do*, and not *I believe the way they do.* Maybe it was the shock of knowing that she was no longer alone in the way she thought and believed. She had arrived alone at her belief that Catholic doctrines were wrong, were not truth, and were not approved by God. Yet, these Adventists were saying that from the pulpit and writing it in their books. *They agree with me.*

When the evangelist gave a presentation on the state of the dead and explained that the Bible teaches that the dead are asleep until Jesus comes and that they are not burning in hell, she thought, *There it is again. They think like I do.* The evangelist spoke about Ellen White and how the Seventh-day Adventist Church views this woman, a prolific writer born in the early 1800s, as a prophet sent from God. She thought, *I've never heard of her.* So, of course, she went to the Adventist bookstore and bought a book called *Counsels on Diet and Foods*, one of the many books that Ellen White wrote.

Once again Laura was astounded. *I know this stuff*, she thought. She read about the dangers of alcohol, tobacco, white sugar, and white flour. Those were the four things she was absolutely convinced were bad for her health. She thought that eating meat wasn't good, but she read literature that presented both sides of the issue and was on the fence about it, even though she became a full-time vegetarian. *Ellen White thinks like I do. And she's got more and better information than I've got.*

Is this the best way for a person to find her way to the truth? Maybe it isn't, but that's how Laura did it. She studied Adventism carefully, and each time she learned something new, it matched up with her own personal definition of truth as she came to understand it.

She had been going to the meetings for about a month and had heard most of the doctrines when she decided she wanted to become a Seventh-day Adventist.

She arrived at this decision all on her own. Nobody approached her at the meetings. That was the way she wanted it: she was just an anonymous face in the large crowd.

She had a couple of problems to deal with, however. Her parents still thought she was a good Catholic. She didn't want to risk being open with them. She didn't lie to them; she just didn't tell them anything about her search for truth. She knew that they would disown her as soon as they learned of her decision to join the Seventh-day Adventist Church. She might never see her mother and father again. As much as she wanted that not to be a problem, it still filled her with dread and sorrow.

The other difficulty was with the Sabbath. Adventists believed that the seventh-day Sabbath should be kept as a day of rest—all of it—not just the going-to-church part. That, of course, meant not working on Saturday. She was new at her job, and although she was making good money, she was expected to work fifty to sixty hours a week. Being on call on Saturday was a requirement of the job, so as soon as she joined the Seventh-day Adventist church the Sabbath would become an instant problem.

She decided that she would wait about two years before getting baptized. On the practical side, that would give her time to get her debts paid off so that she could more easily risk losing her job. She still owed her mother almost six thousand dollars, and she knew her mother would probably demand that it be paid back immediately when she heard that Laura was an Adventist.

Two years would also give her time to start hinting to her parents about her change in religion. Maybe she could help her mother understand that she loved her even though she was leaving Catholicism and that her decision was not meant to hurt her mother in any way.

Actually, Laura was also rethinking her long-range plan to become a doctor. *I'm not so sure that I still want to go to medical school*, she thought. Even though she was working long hours, she really valued her free time. Having her evenings to herself was something she never had in her entire life. Medical school would mean minimal amounts of free time for her foreseeable future and maybe for her whole life.

Money wasn't as important to her as it once was. Maybe that was because what her family thought of her was also becoming less important. But the big question facing her right then was whether she should wait two years to be baptized. Was that what God wanted her to do? She thought it through and weighed all the pros and cons. The sensible thing to do was to wait. She told no one except Melissa about her decision.

The next night after making this decision, she attended a meeting, and the evangelist said something she didn't understand. So she got in line afterward to talk with him, like many other people did. She intended to ask him for clarification on something he had said about the Catholic Church.

The line was long, and finally it was her turn to ask her question. She opened her mouth to speak, but before she could say anything, he spoke to her.

"I am so glad you are in the line tonight. I needed to talk to you. What church are you a member of?"

"I'm not a member of any church."

"Well, what church were you raised in?"

"I was raised a Catholic."

"Oh, OK. I need to tell you that I saw your face out in the crowd on three different occasions in the last couple of weeks, and I was impressed that I needed to talk to you."

How in the world could he have seen my face? Laura thought. *In this huge auditorium, Melissa and I deliberately chose to sit in the back where it's dark. Did my face shine somehow? Was there a light on it or something?*

"I need to tell you that you should give your heart to God and be baptized immediately. Do not wait. If you wait, you will never get baptized."

Laura freaked out. How did he know she had made the decision to wait for baptism? How could he know that she would never get baptized if she waited? This was too scary. It was way too close to her experiences with the psychic, the tarot cards, and the Ouija board.

"I have to go," she said as panic filled her voice, and she and Melissa hurriedly left the building. She didn't ask her question.

"I'm not going back to those meetings," she told Melissa the next night.

"Fine by me," Melissa said. "Let's go shopping instead."

The next night Melissa and Laura drove to the mall in Bakersfield. The mall was surrounded on three sides by busy multilane streets. Laura and Melissa parked on the edge of the parking lot, near one of those streets.

As Laura was getting out of the passenger side of the car, she looked up and saw a blind man with a white cane crossing the road. Then, in the blink of an eye, she saw a car slam into him. The man's body bounced three times before he lay motionless in the road, not more than twenty-five feet from where she stood.

Laura was frozen to the pavement with shock. Her own accident had happened only seven weeks before. As she stood there, she heard an audible voice. It wasn't her own voice. There was no one except Melissa near her in the parking lot, but the voice came from right behind her.

"Take heed," it said. *"You should be dead from your car wreck, and you're not and that man's dead. Don't worry about the obstacles before you. Don't worry about your parents. Don't worry about your job. Those things will take care of themselves. Don't wait. Go get baptized."*

Laura didn't know whose voice she heard. She didn't know how this voice knew her situation. For that matter, she was still puzzling over the fact that the evangelist had seen her face shining in the dark auditorium. She found all this upsetting; but the message was compelling, and she knew what she needed to do. She would get baptized.

The next night she and Melissa went back to the meetings, and they continued to attend every one. Laura spent every available hour reading her Bible. *I've got to read more of this Book*, she thought. *I need a lot more of this great power in my life.* She spent several hours every day reading the Bible and was drawn to the God it described. Everything else in her life receded into the background as she delved into God's Word, often studying, reading, and praying during all her spare time every day.

One night the evangelist talked about the war between good and evil and how it began in heaven and how the war continues on earth to this day. He read from chapter 12 of the book of Revelation about how the devil and his angels fought against Michael and His angels and how the devil and his angels were kicked out of heaven. He said the Bible teaches that they were cast down to the earth and that the devil considers himself the prince of this world.

He talked about how God uses and guides people to do good deeds on His behalf and how the devil uses and guides people to take actions that oppose the good God wants to do and attempts to bring harm to people.

As Laura listened, she thought of the many times in her life when things turned out well; times when she should have died. God must have been involved. God must have used Lois to prevent Laura and Mark from killing their father and going to prison. It must have been God or His angels who gave her the impression not to commit suicide. God must have used the doctors to prevent Laura from dying of kidney failure. God must have worked through the Texas legislature to approve students in their fifth year of college for Pell Grants. God must have been involved in saving Laura's life during the car wreck.

Laura saw how God had intervened many times in her life to keep her alive and bring her to this moment. As her mind was filled with these thoughts, her heart was flooded with the deepest sense of gratitude! She had no words powerful enough to express the thankfulness she felt. This intense gratitude overflowed into a profound love for her heavenly Father and a desire to serve Him. She decided to live the rest of her life doing actions that would express her thankfulness to God; she just didn't know what they would be. All she knew was that she wanted to do a great work for God, and she would trust Him to let her know what it would be.

That night Laura thought more about the lecture on the war between good and evil. She wondered if there were rules of engagement to this heavenly war such as those for earthly wars and if so, what they were. She knew that rules of engagement are typically negotiated between both sides, and they restrict both sides' activities. During the next few days, she studied her Bible to see if she could find any rules of engagement and, sure enough, she found them!

In the first two chapters of the book of Job, she learned from Job's story that Satan can't take actions against one of God's followers without God's permission and that God is restricted in His actions if a person chooses Satan or the side of evil. Another rule she found is that God respects a person's freedom of choice and will not force anyone to do His bidding, and He ensures that Satan is not able to force his will on those who choose to follow God. But for those who don't choose to serve God, Satan has the right to reign over them as their king.

Although God is all knowing and all powerful, the rules of engagement limit His involvement in people's lives if they choose evil over good. Humans have freedom of choice, and their choices are the big deciding factors in their lives.

Laura found these ideas to be powerful because they answered one of her biggest questions: why didn't God answer her prayers as a small child? They explained a lot of the things that happened in Laura's home.

Immediately after encountering these ideas, Laura called her mother and asked if she had ever prayed to God to stop the abuse and suffering that was happening in their home when Laura was young. Mary Sicking replied that she had never asked God for specific help because there is no Catholic prayer for that kind of situation. It had never occurred to her to pray a spontaneous prayer for help.

Laura came to believe that God would have helped her parents if they had asked, but they hadn't asked. Her dad wasn't interested in religion. Laura understood that at the time he didn't want God to be involved in his daily life. So, Laura reasoned, Satan had a right to be in their home because her father may have chosen the path of evil without knowing it. But God also had a right to be in their home because her mother tried to follow God as she understood the truth to be. So the battle between good and evil that began in heaven was waged in Laura's home for the souls of the children!

Laura saw that the choices of her parents took precedence over the prayers of young Laura when she asked God to change everything in her home and stop the hurting. Instead of rescuing Laura from her painful home, God strengthened her to endure it. Laura saw the difficult position God was in. Her study of the Bible brought her to the conclusion that God respects people's freedom of choice so much that He doesn't take actions to prevent them from doing what they want to do, and yet He grieves as He watches the human suffering that results from their choices.

This new perspective helped Laura understand and forgive God for not answering her prayers and stopping her pain when she was a small child. By the age of fourteen, she had been so angry at God that she had stopped talking to Him for ten years; but now she felt her anger melt away as she understood the war between good and evil. So much of Laura's life began to make complete sense as she viewed it through the lens of the rules of engagement associated with that war. Choices are extremely important! And so is praying for other people; it gives God the right to become involved in a person's life because someone is asking for help.

Laura read in the Bible about the children of Israel and how the Lord rescued them from slavery and brought them out of the sorrows of Egypt. That was a story she could relate to. Her heart was touched as she read of God's dealing with the Israelite slaves. She felt that God did the same thing for her. It was the same Lord, the same God, who was bringing her out of the house of her own slavery and setting her free from her sorrows.

She felt drawn to Jesus, the Defender of the social outcast and the compassionate Friend of the poor and lonely. She read more deeply about Jesus' life in a beautiful book called *The Desire of Ages* and was drawn to the Son of God who suffered abuse as she had, even though He was innocent. She felt love growing in her heart for such a wonderful God who would do these things for sinful humankind. Her frozen emotions began to thaw, and she cried as she read of Jesus' loving deeds for suffering humanity.

She read the story of Christ's crucifixion. She saw that He suffered sexual abuse as He hung naked on the cross while surrounded by jeering onlookers. He suffered physical abuse as they spat in His face and beat Him. He suffered verbal abuse as the mob mocked and taunted Him as He hung on the cross. He knew what it felt like to be unjustly accused and to be beaten and abused. He suffered, much more than she had suffered.

Not only that, He suffered in order to give her an opportunity to be saved and go to heaven; He suffered so she could enjoy the wonderful life in heaven that He gave up to come to earth! She grew to love Him and talked to Him every day. He became her best Friend. She found herself crying joyful tears of gratitude and love for such a God who would do these great things for fallen humanity.

One day she came across the plastic bag that held the contents of the wrecked Vega's glove compartment. Inside she rediscovered the little book *Steps to Christ*. She began reading it again; this time, combined with all of the other new things she was learning, it made perfect sense. She cried as she read about the beauty of God's love and goodness.

She began to understand the concept of God's grace; that gift of complete forgiveness and acceptance that Jesus won for her through His suffering at Calvary. She finally understood the power of God to effect change. Her heart was completely melted with love and admiration. *This is the heart of truth, and the most beautiful of all the Christian doctrines*, she marveled. For the first time in her life, she understood why Christ's death on the cross is so very important. Because of the gift of grace, God the Father and Jesus could forgive and accept the emotionally weak side of Laura—the little girl inside her—and not only forgive her but love her unconditionally.

Laura was awestruck at this new insight. *God was the first Person who ever really loved me for who I am*, she thought. As a little child, He was the first One, the only One, with whom she experienced unconditional love. She understood, then, that God loved her and she loved Him in return, but she lost that connection. Now God was teaching the grown-up Laura about true, unconditional love. God was the only unconditionally loving Parent she had ever known. The emotions that were frozen for ten years were thawing.

As Laura read the Bible or heard sermons, she cried as she saw the deep love that God has for sinful, fallen people such as her and for people who may not even like Him. The tears that were bottled up for ten years were being released, and God was healing her heart. To Laura, this was a mighty miracle that no therapist or psychologist could tell her how to achieve!

The Bible called it the balm of Gilead—a healing ointment. God's grace became the balm of Gilead for Laura, healing her suffering heart, spirit, and soul. God's grace was the medication that took away the blackness and cured her sense of her own evilness. It removed the wretched and pervasive lack of her own worth that had burdened her for her entire life. It was such a comfort to read in the Bible that "there is no one righteous, not even one" (Romans 3:10). She realized that everyone is just like her, sinful and in need of forgiveness and of God's power to change, which comes from His grace.

The words of "Amazing Grace," the old familiar hymn, were suddenly filled with new, sweet meaning:

> How precious did that grace appear
> the hour I first believed.
>
> Amazing grace! How sweet the sound
> that saved a wretch like me.

A baptism was planned for December 5, 1981, the last day of the evangelistic series. Adventists follow the biblical practice of baptism by immersion, and a portable swimming pool had been prepared to accommodate the large number of baptismal candidates. Laura was number seventy-six among the many who were baptized that Sabbath. She was white and shaking as she entered the pool.

The pastor of the Bakersfield Central Seventh-day Adventist Church stood ready to baptize her. "Are you OK?" he whispered. "You're shaking like a leaf. What's the matter?"

"You would turn white and shake, too, if you were me," she replied. "It's a long story—too long for now." She was thinking about her parents and the certainty that she would be disowned once they knew. And they would know. She intended to be open with them while recognizing the limitations of what they could handle as well as what she could handle. She was done with living a secret life where no one knew who she really was.

She was wondering how her brothers and sisters would treat her. Would they all freeze her out too? Would she lose her job? Her uncertain future scared her to death, but she knew in her heart that she was doing the right thing. She would let everyone know the real Laura. If they couldn't accept her, she would accept that, or at least try to. Would they walk away from her as she saw them do in her dream about flying?

The cost was extremely high, but she knew there was no other way. God had worked so many miracles in her life to bring her to this point. He had to shake her and make it absolutely clear to her that this was what He wanted for her. Now she knew that this was what she had looked for and strived for her whole life. She had finally found God and truth, and with them, the love, joy, and happiness she had known as a small child. She found God's power to change the undesirable parts of herself. She found everything her heart was searching for.

With God's help, she overcame alcohol. She found happiness—a happiness that overflowed like a mighty river, flooding her heart with joy. That happiness was so precious that she never wanted to be without it again.

The pastor raised his left hand over her head as she gripped his right wrist with both hands. "In the name of the Father, the Son, and the Holy Spirit, I baptize you," he said and then dipped her under the water.

When she came up out of the pool, she was filled with joy. She looked out over the crowd in the auditorium. She spotted Mike and Melissa. Both were wearing big grins. They were so happy for her. Melissa wasn't ready to take this big step herself, but she was happy for her friend.

One sharp pain marred Laura's happiness. Her sister Joyce wasn't there. Laura had called to invite her, got her voice mail, and left a message. Joyce hadn't called her back. She wondered why. San Diego was only a few hours away, and Joyce had left Catholicism herself, so surely she would want to be present at this momentous occasion in her sister's life. Laura knew that Joyce had been concerned when Laura became involved in Buddhism and expected that she would be glad that Laura was becoming a Christian.

Laura was hurt that Joyce didn't attend her baptism. She was looking forward to sharing her newfound love for Christ with the sister who had given her the little book *Steps to Christ*. She was terribly disappointed.

She thought back to the goals she had set for herself when she was fourteen: to become rich, sophisticated, and beautiful. With her baptism, she became rich in the Lord and shared in the untold wealth of His goodness. She became sophisticated, because "the fear of the LORD is the beginning of wisdom" (Proverbs 9:10). And she found the source of inner beauty—a loveliness of soul far more beautiful than any external appearance and a transformation more radical than any plastic surgery could ever accomplish.

With baptism, she finally achieved all of her goals. Regardless of what the future held, she knew she could face it with the courage and strength that comes from the grace and power she had found, her knowledge of truth, and her renewed relationship with the loving, caring heavenly Father she had known as a small child. She had found her resting place and her shelter from the turbulence of life. Fortified by the grace of God, the truth of the Bible, and the precious love of Jesus, she went to bed that night feeling safe, protected, and treasured.

CHAPTER 19

....

"Have You Lost Your Mind?"

Laura's first week as a Seventh-day Adventist Christian didn't go well. On Sunday morning, she took stock of the problems facing her. The first was the need to inform her parents of her baptism. She would write them a long, carefully worded letter that explained everything. She started on the letter immediately, knowing it would take her several days to complete.

Her second urgent problem was the necessity to get Sabbath off at work. She would deal with that first thing on Monday morning. And the third problem was the most pressing: what to do about Joyce. She would call her and find out why she hadn't come to her baptism.

While Laura was imagining this long-distance conversation, the phone rang. It was Joyce. Laura's heart lifted when she heard her sister's voice. Was Joyce calling to congratulate her on her baptism? Joyce's opinion mattered to Laura. Joyce was the only sibling with whom she had an open relationship. Laura admired Joyce for her intelligence and often turned to her for advice. And Laura respected her sister for choosing to leave the Catholic Church and become a Southern Baptist. It gave them something in common.

"Did you really go through with it?" Joyce asked.

"I did."

"What in the world were you thinking? Have you lost your mind?"

Things didn't get any better from that point. Joyce spent the next two hours shouting at Laura on the long-distance line—telling her that she picked the worst church she could possibly choose. There wasn't a worse denomination in the world.

"It's a cult, Laura. It's not based on the Bible. Get out of it." Joyce began quoting Bible texts, then she read something out of a book. Laura could hear the pages turning.

"What are you reading from?" she asked.

"It's a book called *Kingdom of the Cults*. It's by Walter Martin. He is very smart. He has about four PhDs and has done a lot of research into cults. He evaluates and debunks each one, based on whether they go by the Bible or not. And he says this Seventh-day Adventist cult you picked definitely doesn't go by the Bible. It's true, Laura. It's all here in his book in black and white."

Joyce's phone call threw Laura into complete confusion. She knew Joyce well enough to know that she saw everything in black and white. There were no gray areas with her sister, and she always thought she was right. People disagreed with Joyce at their own peril. Laura knew all that, but still . . .

Maybe Joyce *was* right. Maybe Laura was completely fooled. Maybe all the wonderful new things she learned from the Bible were wrong. Maybe the sense of being in a new relationship with Jesus and her heavenly Father was just an illusion.

But what about the power God had given her to overcome alcohol and compulsive eating? What about the car wreck? She should have died in that accident. Only a miracle saved her. What about the evangelist who saw her face shining out of the audience three times? What about the voice she heard when she saw the blind man get hit by a car? What about all those things? No, these weren't wrong. She believed with all her heart that God led her to this point in her life.

But she didn't want to lose Joyce. When she thought about the possibility of being disowned by her family, in the back of her mind there was always the thought, *Except for Joyce.* Joyce was her family. If she lost Joyce, she wouldn't have any family at all.

That afternoon Laura found *Kingdom of the Cults* at the nearest Christian bookstore. She sat down on the floor in a corner of the store and read the whole section on Seventh-day Adventists—every word of it. It was terribly confusing. *I don't think this stuff is accurate*, Laura thought. *This isn't what I learned at the meetings or by reading the Bible for myself. This isn't what Adventists believe. I think this author is putting his own twist on things.*

But she was so new to Adventism that perhaps she couldn't see the problems this author was attempting to present. Laura turned to the chapter in Martin's book on the Mormons. She had studied a great deal about Mormonism in her search for truth and felt she had a pretty good handle on what they believed and practiced. Again she found the same twisted logic on Mormonism. She had rejected Mormonism as false. She didn't need this author's twist on it to convince her of that. *This author isn't objective*, she thought. *He has an agenda and can't be trusted.*

But she still wasn't sure what to do. Joyce's phone call shook her confidence badly. She thought about it for several days, praying like crazy all the while. She prayed night and day, while at work, at home, and wherever she was. She had already burned some of her bridges. By Wednesday of that week, she had mailed the carefully worded letter to her parents, telling them that she had joined the Seventh-day Adventist Church. That Monday she opened the conversation with her supervisor about her need to have the Sabbath off.

Yet, she prayed, "God, please help me know what to do. I need Your guidance. Did I make the right choice?" At the same time, she prayed about asking for the Sabbath off from her job and that her parents wouldn't disown her after receiving the letter. She spent many hours every day in prayer. She was so absorbed in this problem that she couldn't think of anything else. It was hard for her to even perform her duties at work.

Laura had prayed like crazy for about three days when she had another dream. This time she found herself climbing up a very narrow, steep mountain path. Although she saw no other people on the path, it was deeply worn, indicating that many people had climbed it before her. As she climbed higher, the path got steeper and more difficult, forcing her to climb on her hands and knees.

When she finally reached the top of the mountain, she saw a large building. It had a white marble foundation, and there were white marble columns around the outer edge. As she got closer, however, she realized that the roof was gone. Half of the walls were gone. The house was dilapidated. Only the foundation and the pillars looked perfect.

Laura stepped up on the foundation, turned, and looked out over the mountain. She saw the most beautiful view she had ever seen in her life. Spread out below her were exquisite green plains and forests. In the distance, she could see the desert and the vast blue ocean beyond that. It was as though the whole earth spread out below her.

This place is so beautiful, she thought. *There should be thousands of people here to see it.* She turned around to see where all the people were, but there were only three men standing on the foundation with her. They looked like very old men. They wore long white gowns and had long white hair and beards. As she looked more closely, however, she realized that their faces were very young.

"Where are all the people?" she asked. "This is a beautiful place. It is a little hard to get to, but there should be thousands of people here."

One of the men replied, "There are no people here because of the winds. When the winds blow, they're strong enough to sweep you off the mountain to your death."

"What do you do when the winds blow?"

"There is only one thing you can do. You must hold on to the pillars of the house."

As soon as the man stopped speaking, the most ferocious winds began to blow. Laura, in her dream, threw her arms around the nearest pillar of the house, which was only slightly larger around than she was. She had experienced high winds in Texas. She had even gone through a hurricane. But she had never felt winds as strong as these. They were the most ferocious winds she had ever been through. She held on for dear life as the winds lifted her off her feet and her body flipped back and forth.

Her arms and shoulders were filled with pain as she struggled to hold on to the pillar, and she felt her strength fading. "I'm going to have to let go!" she called to the man who spoke to her. "It hurts too much! I can't hold on any longer!"

"No, no! Whatever you do, don't let go!" he shouted back. Then he said, "You don't need to hold on with your own strength. You are not in accordance with the pillar! Line your arms and shoulders up so that you are behind the pillar. The pillar will shield you from the wind."

Laura fought her way around so that she was right behind the pillar. Now the force of the wind was taken by the pillar—not by her own body. She found she was able to put her feet back on the solid foundation beneath her. And as soon as she did, the wind completely ceased.

She stepped away from the pillar and turned to smile at the man in white. "Wow, those winds are amazing," she said.

"Yes, they are strong."

"Are the winds the reason why the house is so damaged?"

"Yes, the winds harmed the house."

"I wonder what it looked like before."

"I'll show you," said the man, and he withdrew a picture from his garment and handed it to Laura.

The picture showed a large, skillfully built log cabin. It looked warm and welcoming. Light spilled out of its many windows, and smoke curled from its chimneys. She could see no marble foundation or white pillars. Laura looked at the picture and then at the damaged building before her. "Wow," she said. "I would never have known these were the same house. It's so sad that the winds have harmed it so badly."

"Yes, it is," the white-haired man replied. "It was very beautiful. And it was special. Anyone could go inside this house, and they would never be hungry or thirsty again."

"You know what?" Laura said. "I have searched for this house all my life. My parents brought me here once when I was very young, but I lost my way. But now that I've found it again, I must go down the mountain."

"Yes, you must go now," the white-haired man said, smiling. "But be sure to come back again."

"Yes, I'll come back again." In her dream, Laura looked down the mountain, and her eyes followed the path where she would walk and saw another foundation. It was just like the one she was standing on, but it was smaller and had no pillars.

"What is that foundation?" she asked.

"That's the foundation of a church that once existed a long time ago, but the winds completely destroyed it."

"Oh, I see. I must go now."

"Be sure to come back."

Laura pondered long and hard about what the dream meant. She prayed earnestly that the Lord would help her understand the meaning of the dream. She came to believe that God was telling her to hang on to the truths that she had found. The Bible truths she believed in were the pillars she held on to in the dream. She was told to line up her life with the pillars and hang on, but it was important that she didn't hang on through her own strength. It was only through God's strength that she would survive. Through prayer and God's power, God would help her avoid getting beat up by the winds of adversity that faced her. God would protect her. She would be safe behind the pillars of grace, truth, and the Bible.

Shortly thereafter, she read 1 Corinthians 3:11: "For no one can lay any foundation other than the one already laid, which is Jesus Christ." Jesus was the Foundation! She would stand strong on the Foundation, and the truth would shield her.

The white-robed man in the dream encouraged her to come back again. Did that mean she would someday face some new, perhaps even more difficult challenges in her life? Although she wondered what the winds of adversity would be the next time, Laura believed that this dream indicated that she was making the right decision. She would remain a Seventh-day Adventist—no matter what it cost her. But then she got another idea. Maybe she could be a Baptist too! She was sure that would make Joyce happy. That way she could keep Joyce's friendship and have at least one friend in the family.

Back on her knees she went, praying like crazy. She wouldn't make any decisions without God's guidance. "God, tell me what to do!" She prayed that prayer for three days, and then she had another dream.

This time she was sitting in the back pew of a church. Her new Adventist friends were there, too, filling the last two pews of the church. Mike was sitting beside her. In her dream, she knew that this was not an Adventist church. It was a Sunday-keeping church—an amalgam of all the various denominations—as though they were blended together into one church.

Her Adventist friends were reading their Bibles. They were talking to each other, discussing what they found in the Bible. Laura enjoyed the conversation, but when a man at the front began to speak, she stopped talking and paid attention.

The man, apparently the minister, stood at the pulpit and preached. He was dressed entirely in black, and his Bible was closed at his side. The majority of the congregation was also dressed in black, and their Bibles were closed at their sides.

The remaining people in the congregation were dressed in cream-colored clothes. These people had their Bibles open and were reading from them. They frequently tapped the shoulders of those dressed in black and attempted to show them something in their Bibles.

The black-clad members of the congregation shrugged them off rudely. "Don't talk to me," they said. "Leave me alone. I don't want to hear it." But the people dressed in cream kept persisting, trying to get the others to pay attention to what the Bible said.

Just then in her dream, Laura noticed a tall man standing by her side, dressed in white slacks and a white shirt. He had short blond hair, strong features, and broad shoulders. His face was gentle and kind. In her dream, Laura felt safe and secure in his presence, as though she was being protected by a loving father. He was so tall that her head barely came up to his chest. She looked up at him and said, "Well, I think I need to go home and put my black clothes on."

"Why would you want to do that?" he asked.

"Look around you. Most of the people are dressed in black; I'm wearing cream and I want to fit in. I need to go home and put my black clothes back on."

"Why? Don't you like your cream-colored shirt?"

"Well, yes, I like it."

"Didn't you choose that shirt yourself?"

"Yes, I did."

"And aren't you happy with your cream shirt?"

"Yes, I'm very happy with this shirt."

"Then, why change?" the tall man persisted.

"Because everybody notices my cream shirt. I stick out like a sore thumb."

"Yes, but aren't you happy?"

"Yes! I'm very happy."

In her dream, Laura turned then and took a good look at the other people in the congregation. The people who were wearing black listened to the preacher as though they were hypnotized into a trance. The people in cream continued to try to get their attention, tapping them on the shoulders and showing them texts in the Bible. The people in black resented this interruption of their trance-like state. They didn't want to be disturbed.

"I think I've learned something here," Laura said to the tall man in white. "I cannot base my faith on what other people say. I must base it on the Bible and the Bible only."

A wonderful smile filled the face of the man in white, and he nodded his head. "Yes."

Laura awoke from that dream flooded with a renewed sense of purpose and peace. She had made the right decision. She would remain a Seventh-day Adventist and a Seventh-day Adventist only, no matter what. She realized that her faith must be based on the Bible and not on other people's opinions.

Now that her decision was made again, she was filled with so much joy, happiness, and peace that it reminded her of the runner's high she used to experience on her long-distance runs. But this was far, far better and much more intense and long lasting. Her prayers were filled with thanksgiving for God's wonderful gift of guidance and grace.

Her letters to Tom overflowed with her newfound joy and contentment. She told him about her conversion experiences, her challenges, and her baptism. Tom left medical school one year shy of getting his degree and was working as a medic for the Peace Corps in what was then Zaire. Even though Tom was in Africa, Laura continued to feel close to him. Tom wrote back that he was happy for her.

There was still a price to be paid, however. Joyce called again, determined to talk Laura out of her decision. This time Joyce was armed with Bible references, and Laura could hear the frustration in her voice as she flipped back and forth in her Bible while searching for the texts. *Joyce doesn't seem very familiar with her Bible,* she thought. She realized that she had never seen Joyce with a Bible.

Then Joyce started in again on *The Kingdom of the Cults.* "I read every word of that book, Joyce," Laura said. "That man twisted the beliefs and doctrines of every religion he talked about. I know that for a fact because I've studied them all myself. I think he has an agenda and is untrustworthy. I'm convinced that the information in his book isn't reliable."

Joyce wasn't going to be put off that easily. She next attacked Adventism for being too works oriented; this was an idea she got from her Southern Baptist pastor.

"Joyce, that just isn't true. Adventists believe in grace! It's at the center of our whole belief system! That little book you gave me, *Steps to Christ,* did you ever read it? It is full of the doctrine of grace, Joyce! That book, by the way, is a Seventh-day Adventist book, written by our prophet Ellen White."

"No! That can't be true!" Joyce was so stunned by this revelation that she was momentarily speechless, especially considering she bought the book in large quantities to give away. Not long afterward, she hung up the phone. That ended their relationship, and Laura didn't hear from her again for more than two years. Laura's sister Deb called her one day, not long after her baptism. "I don't think you have any idea what Joyce is saying about you or how much she has hurt you in this family," she said, going right to the heart of the matter without any pleasantries. Laura knew that it was true, and it made her sad to hear it.

Most of Laura's siblings had abandoned their own religious beliefs in their hearts, although not publicly, and had become particularly prejudiced against born-again Christians. Joyce hid her own conversion to the Southern Baptist

Church from most of her siblings, even while spreading lies about Laura. As her dream of flying predicted, most of Laura's brothers and sisters turned their backs and walked away from her.

CHAPTER 20

....

God, How Important Is the Sabbath?

When Laura made the decision to be baptized, she knew there would be a price to pay at work. The price could be high; she might even lose her job. During that first week of being an Adventist, she was dealing with the doubts that her conversation with Joyce had planted in her mind. Had she made the right decision? She determined to trust God and move forward as though she had. So she forged ahead.

On Monday morning, after her baptism on Saturday, she talked to her supervisor and told him that she couldn't be on call the next Saturday or any Saturday, for that matter. Normally, she worked from 8:00 A.M. to 5:00 P.M. five days a week. But every engineer who worked at the refinery was expected to be available on weekends and nights whenever needed. Laura was regularly scheduled to be on call on Saturdays and Sundays.

Her supervisor was shocked at her request. "Laura, this is a totally impossible demand. You do realize this could cost you your career?" he told her. "I think you need a little more time to consider it. Why don't you think about it for a day or two and then, let's talk again."

She went to see her supervisor again the next day. Bob was a nice guy; he liked Laura and appreciated her work. He wanted to keep her from destroying her future. He shook his head in amazement when she told him there was no way she was going to change her mind.

"Bob, I attended some Bible seminar meetings at the civic center, and I was baptized into the Seventh-day Adventist Church on Saturday." Laura explained all about the Sabbath and that it was kept from sundown on Friday to sundown on Saturday night. "I can't be on call during those hours, Bob," she said quietly.

"This is an oil refinery, Laura. It operates twenty-four hours a day, seven days a week. Nobody gets Saturday off, not even me. Getting every Saturday off is simply an unrealistic request!"

"I recognize that," Laura said. "But nevertheless, I need the Sabbath off."

"Well, Laura," Bob said, shrugging his shoulders and throwing up his hands in exasperation, "this kind of thing is above my pay grade. You're going to have to talk to my boss." He arranged a meeting with his boss for the following day. The meeting was a repetition of everything that happened the day before. Laura explained her need to have Saturday off, and her boss's boss said exactly the same thing: "Nobody gets every Saturday off at an oil refinery. We run twenty-four hours a day, seven days a week." The upshot of that meeting was that another meeting was called—this time with Getty Oil's attorneys.

Laura was told that the attorneys weren't available for several weeks. When the schedule came out, Laura saw that she was on call that Saturday. The only way she was going to make it through without losing her job that weekend would be if the units of the refinery for which she was responsible fell completely apart and were nonoperational on Saturday or if they were working so well that her presence wasn't required.

Once again she was on her knees. "God, please break those refinery units, or make them run great," she prayed. She continued to spend hours in prayer every day, asking for God's help and guidance. That Sabbath, although she was technically on call, she was never called in to work. For the next couple of weeks, God answered her prayers, and she wasn't required at the refinery on Saturday.

Then the meeting with the attorneys took place. Her supervisor and two members of higher levels of management were there, along with two of Getty Oil's lawyers. Laura was asked to be present. The meeting was short.

"Miss Sicking," the attorney spoke directly to her, "the company has reviewed your case and made its decision. You were aware of the twenty-four-hour nature of our work here when you accepted this position. It is impossible for the company to accommodate your Sabbath needs. If you refuse to work on the next Saturday as required, you will be fired immediately." Laura was dismissed, and the meeting was over.

Laura was shaking as she returned to her desk. This was serious! She thought about her fifteen thousand dollars in college debt. How was she going to pay her mother the money she owed if she lost her job? For that matter, how would she ever get another job if she got fired from her very first job out of college? She had no one to turn to and no one who could help her. She was on her own. How would she pay her rent? Make her car payment? Buy her food? What would she do?

Laura continued praying many hours every day, and God took care of the problem. For seven Sabbaths in a row, she was on call but never called into work. Laura relaxed a little and prayed less, but during the eighth week, several units at the refinery malfunctioned.

Bob called her into his office and told her she had the Friday night and Saturday shift that weekend. This was it—the moment of truth. Laura lost her resolve, and she worked a twelve-hour shift, from 8:00 P.M. Friday night to 8:00 A.M. Saturday morning. When she got off work, she was angry at herself for her lack of backbone. *Even though I've worked for twelve hours straight and I'm exhausted, I really need to go to church this morning,* she thought.

Her head was in a whirl as she sat in the pew. Her body ached from the long night of work, and her mind was equally as tired. She sighed. *If I don't have the guts to stand up for what I believe, what is the point? How important is the Sabbath, anyway?* She spent more hours in prayer that Sabbath afternoon. *God, how important is the Sabbath? This is costing me big time. Is it worth the sacrifice? Just how important is it?*

Laura looked through the books on her shelf and began to read everything she could find about the history of the Sabbath. Those who had kept the seventh-day Sabbath suffered for it throughout the centuries, both Christians and Jews. For instance, Sabbath keeping helped the Nazis identify Jews, which lead to their capture, imprisonment, and death in concentration camps.

In another book, Laura read that the Ten Commandments describe the character of God. *I can agree with that,* she thought. *God is love.* She had purchased a poster that depicted the Ten Commandments as they might have looked to Moses (only in English, of course).

The artist portrayed the commandments as carved into two side-by-side slabs of stone that curved at the top. The first slab, or tablet, held the first four commandments, and the second one held the last six. Laura studied the little poster carefully. The commandments on the left-hand tablet dealt with God's loving relationship with humans, and those on the right-hand tablet prescribed how humans should love and deal with each other.

The Sabbath commandment was there in the middle of the list. Laura prayed earnestly, asking God to help her understand whether the Sabbath was important and if so, why. For days, she spent most of her free time studying the Bible and the Ten Commandments, praying all the while.

Then one evening, while studying, praying, and using her analytical skills, something dawned on her: God had put special meaning in the organization and presentation of the Ten Commandments. The first commandment was the foundation for a relationship with God: "have no other gods" (Exodus 20:3).

If a person does not keep that commandment, the natural sequence of events is that he will break the second commandment and build images to other gods, she thought. *If a person breaks the first and second commandments, then keeping the third, don't take God's name in vain, or fourth, keep the Sabbath holy, doesn't matter because the relationship with God has been broken.*

Then Laura saw a similar pattern in the last six commandments. The fifth commandment states, "Honor your father and your mother" (verse 12), and that is the foundation of all relationships between humans. Parents are entrusted with teaching their children what love is. *If a person isn't able to keep that commandment,* she reasoned, *the natural sequence of events is that the children will want to kill their parents, thus violating the sixth commandment, which says don't kill.*

If a person gets to the point of wanting to kill one or both of his parents, then the rest of the commandments don't matter to him, because his foundation for human relationships is broken.

Laura suddenly saw such beauty and symmetry in God's law that she was in awe. *I wonder whether anyone else has ever thought of the commandments in quite this way,* she thought.

Laura looked at the painting of the tablets of the Ten Commandments again. She noticed how the Sabbath—the fourth commandment—was located right at the end of the first tablet as part of the list of the commandments dealing with our relationship with God. It was next to the fifth commandment, which deals with honoring one's parents and is the beginning of the commandments dealing with human relationships.

Was this positioning of the fourth commandment significant? The more she studied and prayed, the more Laura realized that it had a special meaning for her. The central location of the Sabbath in the list of ten indicated that the Sabbath was a special time set aside by God for humans, to give them time for building relationships with Him and with their families and friends. She visualized the Sabbath commandment, set as it was in the middle of the Ten Commandments, as a mighty cable to pull our relationships with God and humankind together.

God understands us, she thought. *He knows we need time to work on our relationships!*

When I read that God is love, what this means to me is that He is a God of relationships—both His relationship with me and mine with other humans. He cares about me and wants me to be happy, and the Sabbath is a symbol of that.

For someone like Laura, whose family relationships were so broken, this new truth about the Sabbath was especially precious. The Sabbath existed to give her time to develop her relationships with God and others. This view of the Sabbath and the Ten Commandments would become the foundation of Laura's efforts to heal all of her relationships.

She knew she wasn't the only one in the world with family difficulties. The world was full of people with broken relationships and broken hearts. God knew how the demands of work and daily activities could crowd out the time needed to mend the brokenness. So He made the Sabbath for humans. He made it the center of the Ten Commandments; He made it the center of the Bible and religion. He made it sacred, and He even added the word *remember* to the commandment—the only commandment to contain that word.

Laura lived every day with the fact that she wanted her father dead. She had even had the urge to kill him herself. As she read and studied the last six commandments in the light of that fact, she saw just how shattered her own relationships with humans were. She understood why she could not let anyone get to know her deeply. She realized that if she was ever going to gain the victory over her inability to develop deep human relationships, she had to deal with her relationship with God first. God put the first four commandments, dealing with His relationship with humankind, in that order for a reason. It was her relationship with God that would enable her to heal her relationships with others.

As Laura delved deeper into the history of the Sabbath, she learned that the day of worship was changed from Saturday to Sunday by the Catholic Church. She was familiar with the fact that the Catholic Church made changes to their doctrines and practices throughout the centuries, but she had never heard this particular bit of history. She didn't need to read more. She was a person with a strong loyalty to truth. She was convinced that the seventh-day Sabbath was the truth. She could see how this truth could help heal her relationships.

The next day a thought came unbidden to her mind: *"You will never know how important the Sabbath is in this life. It is extremely important."*

OK, God, she thought. *I get it. I'm never going to work on the Sabbath again.* On Monday morning, she talked to her supervisor again.

"Bob, I know I caved and worked this weekend, but I can never work on the Sabbath again," she told him. "Do whatever you have to do, but I cannot work another Sabbath." She was praying that he would find her another job in the company—one that didn't require Sabbath work.

"OK," Bob replied with a sigh. "Let me see what I can do." On Wednesday, he called her into his office. "Laura, there are some things going on here at Getty Oil that you don't know about. I'm going to fill you in because I think I might have a solution to your problem."

He told her that she was one in a group of six engineers who were hired directly out of college and all of whom started work in the last few months. The company was so large that Laura wasn't aware of the other hires and had never met them.

"The reason all of you were hired," Bob continued, "was because the refinery was planning an eight hundred million dollar expansion. But now that the price of gasoline has plummeted, Getty Oil isn't going to go forward with their expansion plans. The company is trying to decide what to do with all six of you new hires. Because your university in Texas was on a different schedule than our

California schools, you were the first of the six to be hired, and therefore you have seniority.

"So I'm authorized to offer you another position. I really hope you will consider this. It's an environmental technician position. It would be a three-step demotion, I know, but you would only have to work from eight to five, five days a week, and there will be no on-call work. And even though you would be going down three steps, I'm authorized to allow you to keep your present salary. Please think about it and get back to me, will you?"

Laura went home and prayed about it. It didn't take her long to make her decision. The three-step demotion was troubling, she had to admit. She didn't even want to think about trying to find another job someday after having been demoted three steps, but at least she wasn't being fired. And her salary wouldn't be affected! That could have resulted in a reduction of more than a thousand dollars a month. This was an answer to prayer. God worked it out for her. The Sabbath *was* important. God showed her that by answering her prayers.

CHAPTER 21

....

"Dad's in a Coma, Laura, and It's All Your Fault"

Laura's letter to her parents, which explained in detail why she was leaving Catholicism and joining the Seventh-day Adventist Church, was mailed on Wednesday of her first week as an Adventist. She spent many hours working on the letter and rewrote it several times. She felt relieved when it was finished. This was the first step in the open life she meant to lead from now on.

She knew that her parents would be extremely angry. She remembered her father's violent temper and her mother's cold disapproval only too well. *They're going to need time to cool down*, Laura thought. *I intend to be open with them from now on, at least as much as they can handle, but I'll protect myself by not answering the phone for a few weeks while they cool down.* She decided not to answer her telephone for a whole month. They would have to cool down if they couldn't reach her. Her telephone rang often for the next few weeks, but she ignored it.

Weeks went by; even though she worried about what would happen with her job and with her parents, she experienced a euphoric sense of joy. Peace and contentment stayed with her all day and all night. It was still like a runner's high that never went away. It was just wonderful! Later she came to recognize that special joy as God's way of bracing her for what was about to happen.

At the end of a month, she resumed answering her phone. On Saturday morning, January 2, 1982, at 7:30 A.M., Laura's mother called. As soon as Laura heard her voice, she thought, *Has she really calmed down this much?* Her mother didn't sound angry at all.

"Did I wake you up?" Mary Sicking asked.

"Oh no, Mom. I'm up."

"Oh, are you going to work today?"

"No, Mom, I'm not working today."

"Well, why are you up so early on a Saturday?"

"I am going to church."

"To church? On a Saturday? Why are you doing that?"

Oh boy; she didn't get the letter. She doesn't know! Laura thought. Panic rose in her as a thousand thoughts swirled through her head. *What do I do? I'm not going to lie. Joyce has been covering up her religion for years, and I either have to tell Mom the truth over the phone now or start living a lie like Joyce. I won't do that.*

"I'm not a Catholic anymore, Mom. I became a Seventh-day Adventist a month ago. Adventists go to church on Saturday. I no longer worship on Sunday. I'm not going to be a Catholic any longer. I have made my decision."

"What? Did I hear right?" Mary Sicking's voice changed completely. She was crying and screaming as she continued. "I can't believe you've done this! You're rejecting everything this family stands for! You're no longer a child of mine! You're no longer a part of this family. If you get married, I won't come to your wedding. I don't ever want to meet your husband. If you ever have kids, I don't want to see them either. I don't ever want to see you again. I disown you! You're no longer my daughter! I have only ten children now. And one more thing. I want my money back. All of it. Now!" Before Laura could say another word, her mother hung up on her.

Laura felt intense pain at her mother's raw anger—worse than any physical pain she had ever known. Part of the pain came from knowing that under her mother's display of temper there was something else; a deep and powerful anguish that her youngest daughter was lost to the Catholic Church—lost to heaven—in her mother's mind.

Added to that was the fact that her mother no doubt felt that her own salvation was placed in jeopardy by what she saw as Laura's apostasy. She viewed Laura's decision as her own personal failure. Laura sighed. Her mother's reaction was exactly what she hoped to avoid by sending the letter. For some reason, that letter was lost in the mail, and there was no chance for a cooling-off period.

Laura was the first in the family to openly declare her intention to leave the Catholic Church. Her mother believed that decision would send Laura straight to hell. Laura knew her mother was also concerned that her other children might follow Laura's example.

But knowing the reasons behind her mother's rejection didn't change one bit how made it her feel. She knew that her decision to leave Catholicism meant that she forfeited the love and approval of her parents. She had braced herself for that. She sat in the chair beside the silent phone, shaking, with tears running down her cheeks. She bowed her head and prayed as hard as she had ever prayed.

Fifteen minutes later the phone rang again. Laura wondered what was coming next, but she picked the phone up and answered it.

"Laura? It's Dad." Laura's heart nearly stopped. Her father had never called her before. Never. Not once. And he would never call again. This was the only phone call she received from him during her entire life.

"I don't disown you, Laura. When you come to Texas, stop somewhere nearby, call me, and I will come and see you. I want to see you."

"Oh, Dad, thank you. I will take you up on your offer and stop somewhere next time, so we can meet."

"I don't agree with what you've done. None of your family will ever agree with it. But I don't disown you." The conversation was short, and Laura was soon staring at the silent phone once again, happy for the unexpected support from her father. She thanked God for His answer to her prayer that she not be disowned. At least it was answered with one of her parents.

This was the strangest turn of events possible. When Laura thought about what might happen when her family learned about her baptism, this was the last thing she could have envisioned. As hard as she was trying, with God's help, to change how she felt about her father, she spent her whole life hating him. The whole family hated him. Suddenly, she saw what life with her mother must be like for him, and she realized that she and her father were now in the same boat. They both were rejected and abandoned by Mary Sicking.

Was it possible that she and her father might become friends? Her mother disowned her. Joyce had treated her badly. She was alone. She had no family, except, maybe, her father? Suddenly, her father became her family. *I can't believe I have only one person on my side in this family*, she thought, *and it's my father, of all people!*

Three days later she received word from Joyce that her father was in the hospital in a diabetic coma. He had been told that he was a diabetic five years before, when Laura was nineteen, but had completely ignored that diagnosis and changed nothing about his lifestyle. Now, five years later, his choices had finally caught up with him. But Joyce didn't see it that way.

"Dad's in a coma, Laura, and it's all your fault. You stressed him out with your big announcement about becoming a Seventh-day Adventist, and now he's going to die. What is wrong with you? Why in the world couldn't you have kept your big mouth shut, like me? What good did it do to tell the family and just upset people?"

"I couldn't lie, Joyce. I have to be open with them. I just couldn't lie to them."

"All you ever think about is yourself and what is good for you. Why can't you think about other people once in a while? You're so thoughtless and unfeeling, Laura! You have caused Mom and Dad a great deal of unnecessary pain. If you loved them, you would do what I do, and keep your personal life to yourself.

They need to know very little about your life. You need to tell them what would make them happy. You may call it lying, but I call it sparing them."

"I just can't agree with that, Joyce." Laura felt tired and beaten down by this barrage, but she stood firmly by her decision to tell her parents the truth and live an open life. Joyce kept the truth about her religion a secret to keep their mother's love, but as much as Laura wanted that love for herself, she was through with saying nothing and through with living a secret life and was unwilling to lie. The truth was too important.

Laura prayed many hours a day, asking God to spare her father's life. She was so absorbed in this situation that she couldn't think of anything else. It was hard for her to even perform her duties at work or at home. *I can't bear for him to die now, God! The family blames me for his illness. Please don't let him die, not so soon after he learned that I became a Seventh-day Adventist. Besides, God, You know I have so many unresolved issues with that man. I need time to talk to him. I need him to live!*

Laura continued to pray that prayer for weeks, pleading that God would let Emmett Sicking live long enough for her to talk to him. She got very little information about how he was doing. She tried calling her mother for information, but Mary Sicking continued to hang up on her. She wrote to her mother, and her letters were returned unopened.

Occasionally, Deb would call Laura and give her updates on their father's medical status.

Deb, a nurse anesthetist, was very medically knowledgeable.

Three weeks after he went into the coma, her father came out of it. Two days later he went into congestive heart failure. Laura prayed harder. It was so important that she have a chance to talk with him. Was Satan attempting to kill her father to keep that from happening?

It was a trying time for Laura. She still felt the intense joy that her conversion and her newfound relationship with God brought her, but it was coupled with the nearly as intense pain of her mother's rejection. God knew what she needed, and He gave her great joy to offset the anguish.

Emmett recovered from his congestive heart failure. He lived seven more years, and Laura got the chance she prayed for to work on her relationship with him. For the next seven months, Laura's mother hung up on her every time she called and returned all of her letters unopened. Then Mary's father, Joseph Krahl, died.

There had been a lawsuit over the Krahl future inheritance, which was worth millions, and Mary Sicking was deeply involved in it. This had put a strain on her relationship with her parents. As her relationship with her own mother deteriorated, Mary began to experience the same pain she was putting her daughter through. When Mary called her mother, Grandma Elizabeth hung up on her. When she wrote to her mother, the letters were returned unopened.

Perhaps it finally dawned on Mary that she was receiving the same kind of treatment that she was giving. But whatever the reason, when her father died unexpectedly, she called Laura and asked her to come to the funeral. She made no apologies for her previous behavior.

This call came out of the blue for Laura. It seemed that her mother was extending an olive branch to her. She felt compelled to go, but the funeral was the next day. Laura needed to fly to Texas that very evening. She had only a little more than two hundred dollars to spend. She prayed about it, asking God for help if He wanted her to attend this funeral. With His help, she got the last seat on a red-eye flight leaving that night from the Los Angeles airport. The price of the ticket? Two hundred and ten dollars.

On the flight, Laura imagined what it would be like when she arrived at the funeral, and she felt apprehensive. She would be surrounded by Catholic relatives and immersed in the Old World German culture of her childhood. In that culture, age was meant to be respected. If there was a public confrontation about her religion, her parents would be right by virtue of their age, and she would be wrong. She would be expected to submit to them. The last thing she wanted was that kind of showdown.

She decided that she would not spend any more time at the funeral than absolutely necessary. She left her suitcase and other possessions at Joan's house in Dallas, planning to leave immediately after the funeral and spend the weekend with Joan before returning to California.

At the funeral, however, her dad approached her. "Laura, I would really like to understand the differences between Catholicism and Seventh-day Adventism."

"Dad, I wrote you and Mom a long letter and explained all that. Did you ever get that letter?"

"No, I never saw a letter. Will you come to the house after the funeral and tell me about it?"

This is a wonderful opportunity, Laura thought. It was the last thing she expected, but she knew that her father was intellectually curious. He read widely and loved learning. He was a seeker after knowledge. If he wanted her to explain her religion to him, she would gladly do so.

Her mother made no objection, and Laura was soon back at the farmhouse where she grew up. She and her parents took seats at the kitchen table. Laura noticed that it was new. Other than that, nothing much had changed, and yet everything had changed. She smiled a little inward smile. *She* had changed! She sent a prayer heavenward for help because she had left her Bible in Dallas and had no Bible! *What am I going to do?*

She glanced over at the bookshelf where her father kept his books. She didn't expect to find a Bible there, but perhaps there was something she could use. She was surprised to find a large Catholic Bible.

"Where did you guys get this Catholic Bible?" she asked. "I know you wouldn't have bought it."

"Oh, Joyce gave it to us," her mother spoke up, more than a little smugly. "She is such a good Catholic! We wish *you* were a good Catholic like Joyce." Laura quickly decided that wasn't a good time to tell them that Joyce was a Southern Baptist. She took the Bible down from the shelf and thought, *Where do I start?*

Her father had asked about the differences between Adventism and Catholicism. Both her parents attended Catholic schools for all of their education, and they were familiar with the Ten Commandments. They believed in them. So Laura turned to Exodus 20 and began to read.

When she got to the second commandment, about not making images to any other gods, she paused after reading it through. "Adventists believe this commandment forbids bowing down and worshiping images, such as those to Mary, Joseph, and the saints. We are to worship only God the Father, Jesus, and the Holy Spirit. All others are not gods, and we are not to worship them."

"We don't worship Mary, Joseph, and the saints," her mother began.

"What are you saying?" her father interrupted. "I distinctly remember that you and I knelt before the statue of Mary at our wedding and prayed for eight children to help us work the farm!"

Laura saw her mother's mouth tighten—a sure sign of anger—but she controlled herself and remained seated in her chair.

Laura read the third commandment, then began on the fourth one. After reading it through, she commented, "So the Bible says the Sabbath is to be kept on the seventh day of the week—Saturday. The Jews have kept Saturday as the Sabbath for centuries and still do so, and Jesus was Jewish."

At this, Mary Sicking thumped her fist down on the table and shouted, "Jewish? Jesus was not Jewish! Jesus was a German Catholic!"

Laura's mouth dropped open. She was speechless. *If my mother doesn't know Jesus as a historical human being and His human heritage, how can she ever know Him as her Savior? She thinks He was a blue-eyed, German blond! She wouldn't recognize Him if He walked through the door! Was this what those years of Catholic education taught her?*

Her father turned to her mother and said, "Mary, Jesus *was* Jewish. He was from the House of David."

"Dad, how do you know that?" Laura was surprised.

"Well, to be honest, I've been reading this Bible, and I have a bunch of questions I would like to ask you. First thing I would like to know about is Matthew, chapter 24."

At that, Laura's mother got up and left the room in disgust. Laura and her father talked about the Bible and prophecy for the next several hours. It was a wonderful conversation. When it was time to go, her dad said, "Laura, thank you for telling me what you believe and why you believe it. It is good that you have studied the Bible so carefully and so well. I really appreciate you talking to me about it."

Lois called her one day not long after Grandpa Joseph's funeral. "You deserve to be disowned, Laura," she said. "If I was Mom, I would disown you too." That hit Laura hard, so hard that she called her sister Deb and told her about it.

"Don't listen to Lois!" To Laura's surprise, Deb was encouraging. "I've talked to some of the rest of the family, and we think you needed to make some changes in your life. We can tell you've changed. Joining your church has helped you become a better person. Becoming a Seventh-day Adventist was a good thing for you. Don't let anybody talk you out of your decision or get you out of your church." It was a confirmation of her faith. Her understanding of truth was improving her relationships. Not only that, others were able to see the changes in her.

*   *   *   *   *

Laura's relationship with Mike had developed to the point where he wanted to get engaged. Laura agreed but had some reservations. As time went by, Laura realized that the relationship wasn't working. When she told Mike that she wanted to break the engagement, he seemed oddly happy about it. Shortly afterward Mike informed her that he had been having an affair with a married woman. Despite the fact that she knew they weren't right for each other, Laura was devastated by Mike's betrayal. But then she met the man with the auburn hair.

CHAPTER 22

....

Would You Mind Giving Him a Ride?

Greg Hamilton was the leader of a group of Bible workers. They were teamed up with an Adventist evangelist working in Stamford, Connecticut. Greg spent most of his evenings giving Bible studies. During the day, he worked for a landscaping company to pay his bills. Tall and auburn-haired, he was lean and muscled from his labors, and his redhead's skin was lightly freckled from long hours in the sun.

Twenty-five-year-old Greg was at a crossroads in his life. He knew what he wanted, and being an unpaid Bible worker wasn't the future he envisioned for himself. He had big dreams for serving God, and he prayed often, asking for direction for his life. He was ready to move on to the next stage.

On December 16, 1983, Greg flew home to Bakersfield, California, to spend the Christmas holidays with his family. His parents picked him up at the airport, so he didn't have a car to get himself around during his visit.

Greg's closest friend in town was Jim Buller, who was ten years older. They both attended the Hillcrest Seventh-day Adventist Church in Bakersfield. Greg had known Jim his whole life and considered him a valued adviser. Jim was more than six feet tall, with the tanned skin and ropy muscles of a real outdoorsman. He was the kind of person who loved nature in all of its forms; the wilder, the better.

There was something a little hippielike about Jim. Maybe it was his luxuriant beard and moustache or more likely, his gentle, patient, thoughtful manner. He led small-group Bible studies for the twentysomethings in the Hillcrest church.

The young people, Greg included, looked up to Jim as a spiritual leader, largely because of his deep interest in the study of the life and teachings of Christ and in Bible prophecy.

Laura often attended the Bible-study groups at Dr. Eller's house, where Jim led the study, and had gotten to know Jim and his wife, Becky, well. In fact, Laura thought of Jim as her spiritual mentor and close friend. He became like a big brother to her.

Greg called Jim as soon as he got into town, and Jim drove the twenty-five miles out to Greg's parents' house, picked him up, and brought him to that evening's Bible-study group. He introduced Greg to the other participants, and Laura learned that Greg was the son of her friend Verna Hamilton, who worked at the Adventist bookstore in town. Like his mother, he was friendly, talkative, and an obvious extrovert.

Laura enjoyed the Bible-study group, and she liked to share her thoughts. Greg was also a person who spoke up a lot, and Laura was impressed by his ability to quote from memory whole sections from the Bible and from the works of Ellen White, including the exact chapter, verse, or page number where they were found. It was as though he was seeing the passage in his mind and reading it from memory.

When the study was over, Jim asked Laura if she would mind giving Greg a ride home because his parents lived close by. "Sure!" said Laura, and with that she became Greg's source of transportation for the duration of his visit. She found him very easy to talk to. On that first drive home, she shared her testimony of how she found the Lord.

Greg liked this sincere young woman with the outgoing, friendly personality. He was drawn to this new convert who obviously had a genuine experience with God. He was captivated by her commitment to follow God in spite of the cost.

Greg was a sensitive young man and was blessed with a deep understanding of human nature and human behavior. He was able to perceive the profound sadness hiding behind Laura's bubbly personality—a sadness others couldn't see. He could tell that there was more to her story. He was moved with compassion for her. He knew that with God's help he could be a positive force for good in her life, if she would let him.

Laura liked Greg because he was good looking, and it was obvious that he was incredibly intelligent. It was his mind that first drew her to him. He was also a good listener. She liked the way he gave his full attention to her when she talked to him. She could tell that he was a born leader, but the thing that attracted her the most was the feeling that he was very grounded spiritually. She saw his love for the Lord and his knowledge of the Bible that evening at the Bible study. She sensed that he was a man who knew exactly where he stood in the world and with his God.

Laura knew Greg would be around for only a few weeks during the holidays. She hoped they would be friends. She wasn't looking for another boyfriend. Her experience with Mike was too fresh to even think of such a thing.

By the time they completed the short journey to his parents' house, Greg knew that he wanted to ask Laura out; but there was something he had to do first. He needed to talk to his mother.

"Mom, do you know Laura Sicking?" he asked when he got home.

"Oh sure, we got to know each other in the bookstore. She's one of our best customers. She's bought more Adventist books than most Adventists who have been in the church for years. I know she changed her membership to the Hillcrest church not too long ago, and Ken and I often see her there too. Why do you ask?"

"What would you think about me dating her?"

"By all means, do it!"

Greg had the green light from his mom. He was the kind of guy who dated with the intent to marry, so he wanted to know if she was someone he could consider marrying.

There was a reason for his caution. Greg had his heart broken when his previous fiancée dumped him. The experience hurt Greg badly, so badly that it changed the direction of his life. He dropped out of college and went to Canada. For a while, he was lost, but he spent time deeply praying, studying, and figuring out what he wanted to do with his life. Through a friend, he found work at Sanctuary Ranch, which was an independent mission school in the northern foothills of the Rocky Mountains in British Columbia.

The ranch was primitive by anyone's standards. Electricity and running water were unheard-of luxuries. The temperature could drop to fifty degrees below zero in the winter. Greg was part of a team that built custom log homes from the trees cut down on the property as housing for the students.

He was also asked to teach a class on the life and teachings of Christ. In preparation for that, he spent many hours studying the four Gospels of the Bible and the book *The Desire of Ages* by Ellen White. Altogether he read *The Desire of Ages* through eight times in those years at Sanctuary Ranch.

There in the wilderness, Greg finally figured out who he was and what he wanted to do with his life. Alone in the long, cold, dark winters of British Columbia, he gave his heart to the Lord and made up his mind to give his life to the ministry.

Greg enjoyed working with the students at the ranch. He was good with people. He was a natural leader and had a knack for figuring out what made people tick and how to motivate them. His mother, who was a registered nurse, left her profession and stayed home with her boys when they were kids. She began teaching her young sons about psychology and human behavior when they were only five or six years old, and Greg absorbed this information and put it into practice, even from a young age.

Many of the young people he worked with at the ranch came from difficult home situations and were coping with the results of abuse, neglect, or their parents' broken marriages. They needed more than leadership, and as one of their teachers, Greg learned how to listen to, empathize with, and support them as they worked through their problems.

The four years he spent at Sanctuary Ranch matured his personality and character in many ways. He improved his physical strength, deepened his walk with God, and developed his gifts of empathy and perception.

Greg left Canada after four years and ended up working at Living Springs Retreat, which was an independent health reconditioning mission in upstate New York. It was there that he met evangelist Tony Moore, who invited him to support his ministry by recruiting and leading a team of Bible workers. Greg moved to Connecticut, enlisted several young people, formed a team, and went to work as part of the evangelistic team. He had been working with Tony for about three years when he flew home for Christmas.

Greg now wanted to talk to his good friend Jim Buller about Laura. He needed advice. He liked this young woman—a lot. He was moved with sympathy for her, and he knew that he could help her handle the hardships she was going through. He even knew how to cope with her Catholic family. The neighborhood where he grew up was a largely Irish Catholic community. Many of his childhood friends were Catholics, so he had a pretty good idea of the prejudices Laura was facing. He also knew how to deal with challenging personalities and how to calm the many storms in her life.

But more than all that, he had a feeling that she might be very good for him too. Just before making this trip to California, he had prayed that the Lord would help him find a wife. He wanted to make a fresh start, and he knew he needed a partner to do it. Was Laura the one?

The two men met in a deserted ballpark, and they hunkered down at home plate for the next hour and talked. Jim knew Laura well, or at least, he thought he did. He had been there for her through the whole breakup with Mike, just like he had been there for Greg when his engagement fell apart.

Jim shared everything he knew about Laura with Greg. He knew nothing about her abusive childhood. He had heard the same testimony that Laura told Greg. Greg left the park feeling encouraged about pursuing a relationship with Laura.

Christmas Eve was on Sabbath that year, and Laura went to church as usual. Greg noticed that she was alone and invited her to sit with his family at the potluck dinner after church. She knew his parents and his older brother, Mike, and the family's other friends.

Several days later Greg called her and asked her for a date. Because he had no car, they arranged for her to pick him up. The two drove up to Greenhorn Summit, about an hour northeast of Bakersfield, and went for a hike. At the very top, they found some stumps where they could sit down, and they sat there and talked for hours. They had a wonderful time together, and when Greg came home, his mother greeted him at the door. "How'd it go?" she asked.

Greg was all smiles. "Great!" he said.

"You should marry her," Verna Hamilton replied. So Greg asked her out again the next day. Laura realized that Greg hadn't achieved a whole lot at that point in life, not if she judged him by the world's standards. But he was an intelligent young man with a great personality, who loved the Lord and knew where he wanted to go in life. He was just the kind of friend she needed. It didn't matter that she had more money than he did. Laura thought of her sisters' experiences. *Virginia was right*, thought Laura. *It doesn't matter one bit whether a guy has money or a great education or a terrific job. It's what he is inside and what he can become that counts.* She thought about how her sisters had supported their husbands, putting them through college, and how well it had turned out for them.

Laura also remembered that at fourteen years old she had already visualized what she could become and even started taking steps to achieve it then. She looked at Greg the same way she saw herself then. She saw what he could become, and she also saw that by working as a Bible worker he was already taking steps to achieve it.

On the way home that evening, they were driving along with the car's top down, and the conversation turned to Greg's family. "I like your parents, Greg," Laura said. "Your mom and dad are great." Actually, Laura had known Greg's parents two years longer than she had known him, and she always liked them both, especially Verna, who was so helpful in the bookstore.

"I'm glad you like them so much, Laura," Greg replied. "They like you too. Would you like to join the family?"

Laura burst out laughing. "That's a good one, Greg. Really funny." Greg laughed, too, and let the subject drop. *What was that all about?* Laura wondered, but she put the crazy proposal down as a joke, and Greg didn't mention it again.

After that, Greg and Laura saw each other almost every day. They went for hikes, to museums, and to their Bible-study group and visited with Jim and Becky.

Laura noticed that Greg was very touchy-feely. He took her elbow, laid an arm across her shoulders, and reached for her hand frequently. He wasn't being too familiar or improper. It wasn't like that, but it felt weird to her. In her family, no one touched anyone. It wasn't in their German culture to be demonstrative.

When she thought about it, the touching she remembered from her childhood was in the form of beatings—violent and painful. So physical contact made her uncomfortable. Greg seemed to think it was natural, and after the first time she had dinner at his parents' house, she began to understand why.

His mom was standing at the kitchen sink, and his dad walked in, hugged his wife from behind, nuzzled her neck, and gave her a friendly little pat on the backside. Laura was shocked, but that incident helped her make sense of Greg's behavior. She learned that Greg came from a long line of what she thought of as extremely affectionate people.

I guess I'm a bit standoffish, Laura thought. *I can either learn to adopt Greg's way of showing affection or break off this relationship.* She made up her mind. She would learn to accept it and return it. Although it didn't come naturally to her, deep inside she sensed it was emotionally healthy and the kind of healing she needed.

To Laura, those weeks were filled with carefree, lighthearted friendship; nothing more. She was enjoying their good times together. But for Greg, those times meant much more. He was falling in love.

....

CHAPTER 23

"I'm Going to Move, Then"

Greg's month of vacation in Bakersfield was almost over when he and his parents made a plan to drive up to Fresno to visit Grandpa Duane, the patriarch of the Hamilton family, for the weekend. They planned to go to church with Grandpa Duane, spend the rest of the day and the night at Grandpa Duane's house, and drive home the next morning.

Laura was invited to go along. On the way up in the car, Verna leaned over and said conspiratorially, "Laura, Grandpa is a great guy, but just between us, he can be a little rude and offensive sometimes. Don't take it personally."

She didn't say why he might be rude, but Laura assured her she would not be upset by an elderly gentleman's rough edges. She was confident that she could disarm him and make him like her.

They met Grandpa Duane and Grandma Lou at church. Laura's first thought upon meeting Greg's eighty-one-year-old grandfather was, *He looks just like Colonel Sanders!* His flowing white hair; neatly trimmed moustache and goatee; short, heavy-set build; and his light-colored suit and black tie were very much like the smiling image of Colonel Sanders. Grandma Lou, at about five feet seven inches, was slightly taller than her husband. She had silver hair and thick dark eyebrows that gave strength to her sweet face.

Grandpa Duane's house was small and cozy, located in a quiet Fresno suburb. Sabbath lunch was a well-prepared vegetarian meal served on good china and a white lace tablecloth, and it made Laura feel that she was a welcome guest in their warm and gracious home.

After the dishes were cleared away, the conversation continued around the dining table. Grandpa Duane asked Laura some insightful questions about her life, her career, and her family. She answered in her usual friendly way. She was impressed with Grandpa Duane. He might be eighty-one, but his mind was sharp, and he was obviously an intelligent, wise man. Then the questions became slightly more pointed, and Laura suddenly realized that the rest of the family had quietly faded away. She and Grandpa Duane were alone.

"How do I know you're a nice person, Laura?" Laura was slightly taken aback. Something about Grandpa Duane's tone of voice seemed to turn him from a genial host into a stern interrogator. Without the big smile, his resemblance to the kindly Colonel Sanders had disappeared.

"Well," she stammered, trying to buy herself a little time to think. Usually she was never at a loss for words, but this question seemed to come entirely out of left field. "Well, I found the Lord, and I've given my life to Him. I believe in being a nice person."

"Lots of people who have been baptized are not nice people."

"Yes, I'm sure that's true," she replied. Then she told him her whole conversion story. Grandpa Duane listened impassively. When she was finished, he said, "That's fine, but how do I know you would treat my grandson well?"

The interrogation—for that's what it was—continued for what seemed like several hours. Grandpa Duane continued to ask direct, even abrasive questions, probing into her personality, her motives, and her character. Laura did her best to answer his questions politely, giving him facts about her life, but still he persisted.

This guy doesn't like me, Laura thought. *I don't know why. I don't know what I've done to offend him, but it is pretty clear I'm not going to win him over with my bubbly personality. He just doesn't like me. That's fine. Not everybody has to like me. They can take me or leave me. Clearly, he would rather leave me. So be it.* She excused herself and went into the living room to join the others.

After some time, Grandpa Duane came into the living room, chose a seat across from Laura, and began speaking kindly to her as though nothing had happened.

OK, Laura thought. *He realizes how rude he was to me, and he's trying to say he's sorry without saying it. That's fine.* She relaxed, and the evening continued pleasantly.

The next morning the family was saying their good-byes after breakfast when Grandpa Duane turned to Greg and clapped him on the shoulder. "You can marry her, Son. She will make you a good wife. Just know that when you get into an argument with her, she is not going to stand and fight you. She is going to run off like a little rabbit. You will have to go after her."

Laura was dumbfounded. So that was all a test? She had no idea. She was shocked. But she was even more surprised that she evidently had passed it. "Yesterday you didn't like me," she said. "What made you change your mind?"

Grandpa Duane smiled, looking like Colonel Sanders once again. "Oh, I like you. It was just a test," he replied. "I wanted to see what you would do with conflict." His answer made Laura feel very good. Her initial impression of Greg's grandfather was that he was an intelligent, perceptive man. It felt good to have his approval. Laura learned that an endorsement from Grandpa Hamilton was considered a prerequisite for marriage in the Hamilton clan.

It was time for Greg to leave Bakersfield and return to his job in Connecticut. The holidays were over, but something had changed. Knowing how Greg felt about her made Laura take their relationship more seriously.

They agreed to write to each other, and they did so every day. Greg asked her to fly out to Connecticut to see him for Valentine's Day, and she did. Greg and another member of the Bible workers' team were living with evangelist Tony Moore and rented rooms in the large house the evangelist shared with his family. Laura was invited to stay in the family's guest room. She spent that week doing all of the things she enjoyed doing with Greg in California, including going for hikes and just talking.

The week was nearly over, and Greg was nervously looking for the right time and place to propose to Laura. He found his moment just before she was to fly back to California.

"Laura, will you marry me?"

"Greg, I can't. I'm sorry, but getting married is a big decision to make. We've been dating only a few weeks. I just don't feel that we know each other well enough to make that decision."

"I need to move back to California so that we can get to know each other better, don't I?" he said.

"Well, yeah. I mean I'm not making any promises, but if you are really serious about getting to know me, you need to move to California."

Greg nodded his head and smiled. "I'm going to move, then." In a few weeks, Greg Hamilton was back in Bakersfield to stay.

CHAPTER 24

....

"Laura, Could You Fit Into This Plan of Mine?"

Greg moved in with his brother and got a job selling religious books door to door. He and Laura saw each other every night. He came to her apartment for dinner, or they went to his parents' house for the evening meal. They attended church and Bible studies together, went for long drives, and hiked in the beautiful California hills. Laura enjoyed listening when Greg sang for church. As Greg hoped, their relationship was changing as they spent more time together, and Laura was beginning to think of the possibility of a future with Greg.

One night in May, after dinner, their conversation turned to what they both wanted for the future. Greg had a plan that extended over the next forty years, and he outlined it for Laura. He wanted to go to college, become a pastor, and eventually become a leader in the field of religious liberty. The pursuit and promotion of religious freedom for all people was Greg's real passion, and he saw becoming a pastor as an obvious stepping-stone in achieving his goal.

Laura listened quietly. She had heard Greg talk about his interest in a religious-liberty career before. It was a lofty, worthy goal, and she knew it fit Greg's talents and abilities perfectly. Then Greg asked her a question. "Laura, could you fit into this plan of mine?"

"I could," she replied.

"Well, you know that I need to finish college first. Mom and Dad can't afford to help me. Could you see yourself putting me through college?"

She nodded her head thoughtfully. "I could," she answered again. It wasn't a commitment but more of an acknowledgment that such a thing was possible.

Greg said, "OK," and dropped the subject.

That's interesting, Laura thought. *He didn't ask me to marry him this time. He asked if I could fit into his life goals. That's an important piece. Now we also need to talk about my life goals.*

Laura didn't think Greg's suggestion that she might put him through college was inappropriate or unusual. It was what most of her sisters had done—marrying men without college degrees, and helping them become successful. Greg had every quality he needed for success, and all he lacked was a college degree.

I can see what he could become if I stand beside him and help him, she thought. It was something worth thinking about. And that's what she did; she thought about it and prayed about it. It was only a few days later when Greg brought up the subject of her dreams for the future. "Laura, what are your life goals?"

Laura's perspective had changed since she gave her life to God. She no longer thought of her life goals in terms of her career. Now she saw her profession as merely a way to earn a good living and nothing more.

"God has done great things in my life," she replied to Greg. "I'm not sure what it will be, but I want to do a great work for God as an expression of gratitude." Up to that point, she saw that great work for God as the Bible studies she was helping with and her volunteer position at church, leading out as the personal ministries director. But when Greg described his life goals to her, she caught a vision. Perhaps the great work God had for her was to be a supportive wife in a marriage with a godly man and to work in pastoral ministry. She could see that her life goals and Greg's were complementary and that together they could be very effective in God's work.

She imagined herself as a pastor's wife, giving Bible studies and doing evangelism beside her husband. Of course, she had no idea what being a pastor's wife entailed, but in her mind's eye, she could see them working together, side by side, to spread the gospel. She wanted to go slowly with Greg. But that picture was beginning to form in her head, and the more she thought and prayed about it, the bigger the picture grew. It was a beautiful image, and the possibility that it might become a reality filled her with happiness.

Greg already knew that he loved Laura, and he wanted very much to be her support and strength through life. He admired her intelligence and drive and the feisty persistence with which she forged ahead to obtain her education in spite of the obstacles.

He thought about his own family history. None of the men in his family completed their education—not his father, not his grandfather, and not his brother, Mike. Grandpa Duane wanted to become a minister. As a young man, he enrolled in the theology program at Pacific Union College (PUC) in

Angwin, California. Only three weeks into his college career, his hot temper got him into a fistfight, and he was unceremoniously kicked out of college. He never returned and ended up supporting his family by selling pharmaceuticals.

Greg's dad, Ken, had the same ambition: to be a minister of the gospel. He enrolled in the same school and completed two years of his studies, then changed his major to secondary education. He married Verna in his junior year, and they planned a rosy future together. But then she got pregnant, and Ken had to drop out. He never returned and never got his degree. Like his father, he ended up selling pharmaceuticals.

Greg's older brother, Mike, had a different career in mind. He wanted to be a doctor. He completed his college work and was accepted to medical school. But then his young wife decided that she didn't want to go to medical school with him. She left him and took their baby. He had no idea where his family disappeared to, so he dropped everything and went in search of them, abandoning his education and plans for medical school.

Greg was the family's last chance for educational success. Their hopes and dreams were pinned on him, and he enrolled in the theology program at PUC more to please them than because of any strong desire to be a pastor. His parents and grandparents were overjoyed.

When Greg's breakup with his fiancée led him to drop out after only a year, his family was brokenhearted. When he took off for Canada and found work in a tiny, independent school deep in the wilderness, their dreams were shattered further, and his relationship with them—especially with his father—became even more difficult and strained.

Greg keenly felt his family's disappointment in him. He knew that their concern about his situation was tied up with their own regrets and that he couldn't allow them to control his life, but that didn't make it any easier.

It took him seven long years, but now everything had changed. He shared their ambition for him. He wanted with all of his heart to return to his studies; not to please them this time, but because, with God's help, he now had a vision for his future. But other things changed as well. His parents were seven years older, and they were ready to retire. They no longer had the money to support his dreams.

Laura, of course, had already finished college and had begun her career in a well-paid profession. They knew she valued a college education and would want the same for Greg, if Greg and Laura were married. That was one of the reasons Greg's parents viewed her in such a positive light. His parents' love and respect for Laura was already healing his relationship with his dad. Was it possible that Laura could love him enough to support him while he got his education?

He remembered his prayer from the night before he left to come to California for Christmas vacation. He prayed for a wife, and he had the impression that he would meet her on this trip. He had to admit that he was hoping he would. And now, in Laura, he believed that he had.

It was July 25, 1984. Greg and Laura had known each other for about seven months, and Greg decided the time was right. It was now or never. He suggested they go for a hike up to Greenhorn Summit again. He picked Laura up in his yellow pickup. They drove to the park and made the hike up the mountain. When they got to the clearing at the top, they sat down side by side on the same tree stumps in the same beautiful spot as before. The sun was shining, and the air was brisk and cool.

Greg turned and looked into Laura's eyes. "Laura, I love you with all my heart. Will you marry me?"

"Yes, yes, Greg, yes, I will!" Laura threw her arms around his neck, and he pulled her close. Then he held her at arm's length, still looking into her eyes, and said, "There's something I want to do. I want to sing to you." He cleared his throat a little nervously, but then that beautiful tenor voice soared into the clear mountain air. He sang "Together in Him." "We can climb any mountain, cross any river, as long as we're together in Him." It was a beautiful moment, and Laura wanted to reciprocate. She sang the hymn that seemed most appropriate to her for that moment, "Come, Thou Fount of Every Blessing." "Tune my heart to sing thy grace; streams of mercy never ceasing, calls for songs of loudest praise."

Back in her apartment that night, Laura lay in her bed, filled with happiness and anticipation, but waiting for the pains to start. Severe stomach pains had followed each of her previous engagements. Would it happen again? Nothing happened that night, nor did the pains appear the following day.

Laura thought long and hard about this. Why wasn't she having pain? She knew she hadn't wanted to marry any of the previous men she dated. Their life goals didn't align with hers. Each one had pressured her repeatedly before she agreed to become engaged.

Greg was different. He was persuasive, but he never pressured her to marry him. She was free to make her own choices, seeking God's guidance at each step of the relationship. This engagement was in agreement with her own desires for her life and with what she believed to be God's plan. Thus, no pain!

CHAPTER 25

....

"Let's Go Visit Them Together, Honey"

Just months after Laura and Greg were engaged, word came that the petroleum giant Texaco bought out the Getty Oil Company. It was a scary, tense time for the employees at the refinery. They watched what was happening as Texaco took over other Getty facilities. Hundreds of employees were laid off as the management made sweeping changes in the organization.

Laura's fellow workers were afraid for their jobs. Laura saw the handwriting on the wall and began putting out résumés all over the place. She knew she and Greg needed to move anyway. They wanted to be near a university; ideally, an Adventist one so that Greg could go back to school to study theology. She applied for environmental engineering jobs in all of the cities with a reasonable proximity to these universities. The kind of work Laura did was available only in major cities, and Adventist schools weren't always located near large cities, so she spread her net wider to include the entire United States.

Laura and Greg prayed about it, and she made the decision that she ought to apply specifically for government jobs because government employees worked a regular five-day week, thus eliminating any Sabbath problems. She applied everywhere she could think of and waited for responses.

Then one night she had another dream. This time she dreamed she was sleeping. The tall man with the short blond hair and the strong features—the same man who appeared in her other dreams—appeared by her bedside and woke her from her sleep. Just as before, he smiled at her reassuringly, as a loving, caring, father figure, who was filled with concern for her.

"Laura, God has a new job for you. You are going to lose your current job in one month. You will be unemployed for four months, but then you will get the job that God has selected for you. You'll be moving to a new location. In the meantime, use your time wisely; use your money wisely; and know that God is with you."

Laura woke up from her dream. She had no doubt that God sent this message to her, and she had no difficulty understanding its meaning. She relaxed about the future. Her mind was at ease. God knew what He was doing. He would take care of her employment worries. Exactly one month later, to the day, she lost her job. It happened only two months before her wedding. Four months later, just as she was told in the dream, she found a new job. It was comforting to know that God was so considerate of her. He assured her that she would find a new job in spite of her three-step demotion.

Meanwhile, there was a great deal to do as Laura planned her wedding, but there was one thing that she needed to take care of first. It couldn't wait. For years, she had been writing to her friend Tom. She treasured their long-distance relationship. Now Laura wrote Tom to tell him that she was engaged to marry Greg and that she would no longer wait for him. She didn't hear back from Tom for some time. She later learned this was due to a serious illness he developed in Africa. When he was finally back in the United States, he called her, and they had a wonderful conversation. Tom congratulated her, and they said their good-byes.

Since her grandfather's funeral, Laura's mother had thawed slightly, and they talked occasionally on the phone. Laura always initiated the calls; and they would start off pleasantly enough, but her mother would always make sure that the conversation turned to religion. When it did, the calls became tense.

"Someday you'll come back to the true church of God," her mom said one day, right out of the blue.

"Mom, as long as I read the Bible, I'll never be able to do that."

"That's what's wrong with all you Protestants! You read the Bible too much! Put that thing down, and go talk to the priest. He'll tell you what truth is!"

"I can't do that, Mom."

"I know it!" her mother shouted and hung up on her. But Laura persisted with the calls. She was not willing to let the relationship die.

Now that she and Greg were engaged, Laura called her mother to break the news. "Mom, I'm engaged to Greg Hamilton. He's from California, and he's a Seventh-day Adventist like me."

"Well, you know I won't be attending your wedding, then."

"I know that, Mom."

"If you're not married in a Catholic church, you won't be truly married. A Catholic wedding is the only wedding that matters. You will be living in adultery."

That is so sad, Laura thought. She hadn't expected it to be any different, but it hurt anyway. Laura called her siblings and invited them to the wedding.

Since Joyce's phone calls after Laura's baptism, they had been estranged. Laura didn't try to call her, but Joyce called Laura a few weeks later. She had heard about the engagement through the family grapevine, and she was all sweetness and light.

"Laura, I'm so happy for you! Please let me be your matron of honor!"

Laura was speechless at this sudden turnaround. When she reported this conversation to Greg, he was delighted that her sister wanted to be in their wedding. Perhaps it would make up just a little for her mother's refusal to come. Greg knew how much her mother's rejection continued to hurt Laura, and he put his arms around her and held her tight. "If your mom and dad won't come to us, we'll go to them. Let's go visit them together, honey." And that is what they did. Thanks to Greg's great people skills, it was a big success.

Sunday, December 30, was a sparkling California day. The main sanctuary of the Hillcrest Seventh-day Adventist Church was filled with people. They sent out five hundred invitations, but many went to friends who lived far away. Laura invited all of her family members, including uncles, aunts, and cousins—knowing that none of them would come. Greg's family was small. They expected no more than 100 or possibly 150 guests, but somehow more than 350 friends and family members came.

It was a big wedding. Laura wanted a small chapel ceremony, but when Verna Hamilton heard that, she was dismayed. "Oh, honey," she said to Laura, "if it is an issue of money, please let me help. I've been saving for twenty-five years for Greg's wedding!" Not wanting to disappoint her, Laura allowed the wedding to grow into a large affair.

Laura had two attendants: Joyce and her best friend from church, Jodie. Greg's groomsmen were his brother, Mike, and his close friend Jim Buller.

Laura asked Grandpa Duane to escort her down the aisle. She and Grandpa Duane had grown to love each other, and it pleased him very much to be asked. In his silvery tuxedo, he walked Laura down the aisle on his arm. She looked tiny but beautiful in her long, white, size-four gown.

Greg, dressed in a white tuxedo, stood at the altar, with Mike and Jim beside him. Greg was pale, however, and Laura knew he was fighting a cold, the flu, or something. Jim didn't look too well, either. He had slipped in the bathtub that morning and broken three ribs. The pastor who was to marry them had hurt his back, so the assistant pastor, David Acosta, had to step in to perform the wedding. And to top it all off, the flower girl was recovering from chicken pox—the spots were still visible on her little face. (Much later, Laura reflected on the misfortune of the four people who were ill at her wedding and how it seemed to forecast the health problems she would face in the future.)

The vows were said. As the newly joined Mr. and Mrs. Greg Hamilton turned to face the congregation, Laura was filled with gratitude for the grace and love of God, who brought her from her old life of pain to this beautiful moment.

Laura sold her little Datsun roadster to pay for a two-week honeymoon in Hawaii. The couple traveled to Oahu, Maui, and Kauai and had a wonderful, tender time together—a fitting beginning to a happy marriage.

As soon as they returned from their honeymoon, there was something the young couple needed to do. It was time to deal with Laura's mother's wedding gift, which had arrived just a few days before the wedding.

Mary had sent Laura a ten-dollar check, accompanied by a short note. The letter was dripping with venom, with nothing congratulatory about it. "Here's your wedding present," she wrote. "I want you to know that I will not view you as married, because you aren't getting married in a Catholic church. Don't expect me to be nice to your husband. He'll get the same treatment you do."

The note and the spitefulness of the ten-dollar check made Laura both sad and furious. Their visit to her parents' house in Muenster had gone so well that it raised her hopes that their relationship might improve. This "gift" made it clear that she was dead wrong to hope for any change.

So as soon as they returned from Hawaii, Laura placed a call to her parents from their new apartment. Her mother answered the phone. "Hi, Mom," Laura said as cheerfully as she could manage. "We just got back from our honeymoon. The wedding was beautiful, Mom. There were about three hundred fifty people there. Greg and I wish you could have been there, too, but we understand why you couldn't. Thank you for your note and gift. Have a great day, Mom!"

Her mother was speechless. She couldn't say one word—not even good-bye. Laura quietly hung up the phone and walked into Greg's arms. He held her close as the little girl inside her cried.

CHAPTER 26

....

"You Don't Love Me!
I Remember Everything!"

When the newly married couple returned from Hawaii in mid-January, they took up residence in a small apartment in Bakersfield. Laura, now out of work, continued to send out résumés to state and federal agencies throughout the United States. She applied to companies located near Adventist universities, but these résumés were forwarded to other locations in larger cities. There simply weren't any available jobs in her field in towns near Adventist schools. Finally, she was able to set up two interviews: one with the United States Environmental Protection Agency, at a regional office in Kansas City, Missouri; and the other with the Oregon Department of Environmental Quality in Portland, Oregon. Both interviews went well, but it was Oregon that offered her a job.

By March, Greg and Laura had found a nice three-bedroom apartment in Beaverton, which is a pleasant, upscale suburb of Portland. Laura started her new job, and Greg enrolled in the communications program at Portland State University. The new couple settled down to the business of being married and getting to know each other's quirks and foibles.

They joined the Beaverton Seventh-day Adventist Church—a congregation that was heavily involved in doing evangelistic outreach. Greg's talent as a speaker was soon recognized, and he was invited to conduct a series of evangelistic seminars at the church. It wasn't long before he became a licensed lay preacher for the Oregon Conference of Seventh-day-Adventists. He and Laura worked side by side; he led out in the seminars, and she handled registration and other hosting responsibilities. At the end of the first seminar series they did together, three people were baptized and joined the Beaverton church as members. It was Laura's dream come true: doing a great work for God by sharing the gospel message of God's love and grace, and doing it with the man she loved.

Laura's work at the Oregon Department of Environmental Quality was in the state's hazardous-waste program. She was responsible for inspecting facilities that generated or recycled hazardous waste in order to write the permits they needed to operate. These facilities ranged from factories that refined and produced metals, such as hafnium and titanium, used in F-16 fighter aircraft to companies that specialized in recycling hazardous waste, including dry-cleaning solvents and batteries containing mercury and lead.

Laura spent days, even weeks, in these facilities, analyzing their processes in order to inspect their compliance with laws and write the permits they required.

The likelihood of exposure to unsafe levels of toxic substances was extremely high, but this concern wasn't on anybody's radar at the time. This was in the era before scientists had determined how dangerous such toxins could be to human health. At one of the companies Laura visited, people became sick and were hospitalized because of accidental exposure to contaminated air. This location eventually became a Superfund site because the area was so polluted with hazardous waste substances that federal money was required to clean it up. Laura hadn't heard such concerns discussed on the job or in her chemical-engineering classes. The need for protective garments wasn't yet recognized.

After nearly a year on the job, Laura began to lose weight and develop a wide array of health problems, including a furious appetite, insomnia, general muscle weakness, diarrhea, and allergies to nearly everything. She would take a bite of an apple or a peach, and her body would react with violent coughing. If she continued to eat, she would cough up blood.

Laura was scared. She felt as though she was dying. She did what anybody in her situation would do and went to see her doctor. The doctor referred her to a specialist, who referred her to another specialist. During the next several months, she saw more than twenty-five doctors in all. The doctors ran multiple tests, but none were conclusive.

The last traditional medical doctor she visited was baffled. "I don't know what this is, Laura," he told her. "But whatever it is, it is using up all of the nutrients in your body. If you don't figure out what is going on, you'll be lucky to live another ten years. I've done everything medical science typically does in cases like yours—all of the tests and diagnostic studies. There's nothing else I can offer you, except to wish you good luck in figuring it out." And with that, he dismissed her.

Laura began to explore alternative medicine. She turned first to the Bible and Ellen White's writings on medicine and then to various medical research studies. She found a type of medicine that used a special German diagnostic machine. Through this process, she was able to identify that severe chemical exposure, among other things, was causing her health problems, and she discovered what she needed to do to eliminate these issues. Using this information, plus a careful and thorough application of the eight natural remedies as outlined by Ellen White, her health was restored. In the process, she came to a deeper understanding of how very wise those eight natural remedies are.

*   *   *   *   *

Late one afternoon Laura received a call from home. Her father had had another episode of congestive heart failure. Her sister Deb said it was extremely serious this time. He recovered enough while in the hospital to go home, but his doctors told him he had only a short time to live.

Emmett Sicking's health had been deteriorating for some time. After his first episode of congestive heart failure, which occurred shortly after Laura was baptized into the Seventh-day Adventist Church, he had other serious health scares, including one while his youngest son, Bill, was living at home. At 4:30 A.M., Bill happened to wake up early. He was responsible for milking the cows every morning, but this was half an hour earlier than his usual rising time. Mary's job at a deli required her to be at work by 3:00 A.M., so Bill and his dad were the only people in the house.

Bill walked sleepily with bare feet to the kitchen for a glass of water and was startled to see his father at the kitchen table. His dad was sitting up very straight, clutching the table with both hands; his face was straining as he was unable to speak and was gasping for breath.

Bill took one look at his father's gray face, then ran out the back door and straight to the workshop, where he grabbed an oxygen tank from a welding machine and rushed back into the kitchen, opening the tank's valve as he ran. He sprayed oxygen in his father's face until he could breathe again. Then he called 9-1-1. Bill no doubt saved his dad's life that day. When Laura heard this story, she was convinced that God wanted her father to live until she was able to speak to him about her childhood.

Hearing the news of this latest health scare, Laura wanted to go to Texas. "Greg, I have to see him before he dies! I really need to talk to him about my childhood." When Laura first gave her heart to the Lord, she asked God to help her forgive her father, and she was given the grace to do this. But she knew that step was only the first one on a long road toward her complete recovery.

Laura and Greg flew to Texas and visited her father. Emmett Sicking lay in a large bed in the center of the bedroom. A bedside table held all the usual items: his tobacco tin, his pipe, an opened bottle of Coke, and a stack of books.

She glanced at the carpet. Beside the bed were the normal ashes and tobacco slivers. Other than that, the room was clean and orderly. Her mom, who was still working at the grocery store deli, was also doubling as her husband's nurse.

Laura was saddened by her father's appearance. It was obvious that the reason he was at home was not because he had recovered, but because he absolutely hated hospitals. Emmett didn't like to do what the doctors told him to do. He hated the diets they tried to put him on. He never complied with any of their recommendations. Deb got a peek at his chart while he was hospitalized. In it, the nurses wrote, "Recalcitrant and noncompliant." That was her dad, all right. *No doubt*, Laura thought, *they couldn't waste time and resources helping a person who didn't want to help himself.*

Laura and Greg pulled up chairs close to the bed, sat down, and tried to talk with him. Although he was weak, he seemed glad to see them. "Dad, we heard you were really sick," Laura said. "We came to visit you. They told us the doctors said you don't have many days to live."

"Oh yeah? What do those idiots know? They told me the same thing ten years ago, and I'm still here! I'm just fine!"

Laura didn't know what to say next, so she let Greg carry the conversational ball. He was good at it. Greg and her father were soon chatting away. Laura and Greg stayed at a hotel nearby for several days and visited her dad every day. Laura was upset about how their visit was going. Her desire to talk to her father about his abuse went unfulfilled, and Laura and Greg returned home.

Emmett Sicking recovered from that episode of congestive heart failure; but he did nothing to improve his medical condition or change his eating habits, and it wasn't long before another episode followed. Once again he was given only days to live, and once again Laura and Greg made the trip to Texas to talk to him, staying at a hotel in town.

And once again, although they spent several days visiting and talking with Laura's father, Laura was unable to bring up the subject that she wanted to talk about, even with Greg at her side to provide loving support. She knew there was more to it than just telling her father that she forgave him. She needed to see his face when she spoke of the beatings she and her siblings had endured. She wanted him to acknowledge the abuse he had perpetrated and accept her forgiveness. She wanted to heal their relationship and give him the opportunity to experience the same unconditional love that she did with God and Greg. She was convinced that both of her parents had never experienced unconditional love and were unable to give what they had never known.

She needed to know whether her father knew what he had done and whether he was sorry for it. But the words stuck in her throat. No matter how hard she tried, they wouldn't come out of her mouth. Once again she and Greg left for home without raising the subject and both feeling emotionally exhausted.

Emmett's health continued to be precarious. He went into congestive heart failure again, and several months later he had an episode of kidney failure. Laura was convinced more than ever that God was keeping her dad alive until she could find a way to talk to him. God had given her nearly six years at that point, from the time of her baptism, to come to terms with her abuse, confront her dad, and tell him that she forgave him. Somehow she had to overcome her reticence and talk to him!

The more she prayed about it, the more she came to the conclusion that part of the reason she found it so difficult was that Greg was with her. He was good at keeping the conversation going and a great emotional support! But she needed to do it alone.

Perhaps she also needed to be in the place where the abuse happened. She decided to stay in the house where so much pain had occurred and remain there without Greg until she could come to terms with her memories. Then, through God's power, she would overcome them, speak to her father, and put the matter to rest.

So that is what she did. Laura went to Texas alone, stayed at her parents' house, and immersed herself in the situation, and in her parents' lives. She spent hours talking with her father.

Her strategy was to try to build a rapport with her father and to become friends with him. Her plan was to overcome, with God's help, the pain, the hurt, and the damage in the very place where it happened. She would take the whole week, if necessary, to get to the point where she could talk with him about the abuse.

Laura arrived at her parents' doorstep alone. Her mother greeted her in a friendly way, and Laura was soon seated at her father's bedside. They talked for quite a while. When he grew tired, Laura left the room and visited with her mother while her father napped. It was getting late that evening when her mother raised the question, "Laura, aren't you going to a hotel tonight?"

"No, Mom, I would like to stay here with you and Dad. I've arranged my schedule to stay with you all week, if that's OK."

"Really?" Her mother appeared surprised. None of her children ever stayed in the house. Laura had not stayed in that house for a single night since she graduated from college and could afford a hotel.

Laura stayed in her old room, in the same large space with two double beds where she once slept with Deb, Lois, and Julie. She fitted herself into the routine of the household, and every day, while her mother was at work, she spent hours talking with her father.

They talked about everything. They discussed the books he had read, politics, and the intellectual stuff he enjoyed. Her dad was smart, well read, and a great conversationalist when the talk was on a topic he enjoyed, and he thrived on the opportunity to share his thoughts and ideas with his daughter.

As they grew at ease with each other, Laura began to tell him more about herself and about the woman she had become. She told him that she wrote poetry and read him some of her poems. She said that she loved to sing and, at his request, softly sang several hymns to him, including her favorite, "Amazing Grace." She shared that she loved to read the Bible and read him some of her favorite Bible passages. They talked about the Bible, and both shared things they read in other books as well.

Laura, now quite relaxed with her father, chatted on about Greg, about her job, and about their life in Oregon. The days of that week fell into a pattern. They talked for a while, and then Laura left him to rest for an hour or so and then returned to talk again.

Laura spent most of the evenings that week with her mother. Mary still resented Laura's decision to leave the Catholic Church, but as long as the conversation stayed away from religion, all went well. So Laura did her best to steer her away from that uncomfortable topic.

As she hoped, she was getting to know her father as a friend for the first time, and he was getting to know her. As they shared their ideas and interests day after day, they were developing a friendship. They achieved a level of communication that they never had before.

On the fourth day, Laura felt that the time had come. They had gotten to know each other well enough so that she could finally bring up the abuse and tell him that she forgave him for it. Yet she struggled with how to do it. How could she tell him that she no longer hated his guts and that she no longer wanted to kill him? How in the world could she do that? How could she tell him she forgave him without going into painful detail about what she was forgiving him for?

In the end, she decided not to enumerate his wrongs. Her father knew what he had done. He knew that all of his kids hated him. A man who lives with the fact that four of his eleven kids have told him to his face that they wanted to kill him knows how much he is despised and why.

They were chatting affably when Laura took a deep breath, looked her father in the eyes, and said, "Dad, I have something to say to you—something I want you to know." That got his attention.

"Dad, I want you to know that I love you."

Her father's expression went from relaxed camaraderie to stunned disbelief. He started to laugh a harsh, unpleasant laugh that was full of agonized self-loathing. His next words seemed to be torn from the deepest part of him.

"You don't love me! I remember everything! And I know you don't love me!"

Laura had imagined, over and over again, how her father might react, but she wasn't prepared for this kind of response or for the agony in his voice.

"Look, Dad, I've learned that if I want God to forgive me for hurting others, I must forgive those who have hurt me. And I do love you!"

Her father's face was still filled with total disbelief. He obviously couldn't believe his ears. "OK, Dad, look. I flew all the way from Portland and took a whole week off from work just to be with you! I'm here because I care. I do, I care."

It was obvious that her father needed time to think about this. Laura had spent months thinking this process through and preparing for it. He, too, needed time to deal with what was happening. She felt satisfied. With God's help, she finally told her father that she loved him. When he said, "You don't love me! I remember everything!" she understood that he knew what his abusive behavior had done to her and to their family. His very tone of voice told her that he hated himself for the damage he caused.

Their conversation might have been brief, but she felt strongly that she offered him forgiveness, and he acknowledged his wrongdoing and accepted her forgiveness. This was a big step, and a huge load was lifted off of her shoulders. She relaxed again and enjoyed the remainder of her visit with her parents.

When it was time to go, she hugged both her mom and her dad. Hugging her parents was a new behavior for Laura, but she was determined to do it. She had learned from Greg and his family that hugging was healing.

It was shortly after this breakthrough visit that Laura's parents sold the farm and moved to a house in Gainesville, Texas, nearer to her mother's place of work. Her dad, no longer able to manage the farm or his gravel business, sold all of his equipment and applied for Social Security disability benefits.

At Christmas that year, Greg and Laura sent both her parents a large box of Christmas presents. In her family, this was a break with tradition. Only one present was expected or given. Greg's parents gave each other and their kids multiple presents. Laura liked this idea, and she and Greg bought and wrapped a lot of presents, especially for her father. There was a raccoon cap from Canada, sugar-free candies, several books especially selected for him, and other items.

They called and talked to Laura's parents on Christmas Day. "Dad, did you get your box?"

"Yeah, I got it."

"How did you like your presents?"

"Well, I loved them. I'm wearing the raccoon hat right now!"

"We sent you all those presents because we wanted to spoil you, Dad. Do you feel spoiled?"

"No, I'm not spoiled at all!"

"Well," said Laura, laughing, "I tried! I just wanted you to know how much I love you!"

Her father began crying. "I gotta go!" he said; his voice was thick with tears. "I can't stay on the phone. I gotta hang up!" And the phone went dead.

Laura knew she had gotten through to her father. She pictured the love she showed him as a tiny seed, taking root and growing toward the light, then breaking through the dry, parched soil of his heart. On Father's Day, she and Greg sent him a beautiful card with a check inside and a note that it was to be spent on whatever he wanted. She called again to tell him that she loved him. Once again he started crying, but this time he stayed on the phone. "How can you love me, Laura? I remember everything! How can you say that to me as a father on Father's Day?"

"Dad, I do love you! I learned things from you as your daughter. You taught me what it meant to work hard. That's a very good thing, and I've found it helpful in my life. It has helped me to succeed! Look, Dad, you were the best father you knew how to be, given the resources you had. I love you, Dad!"

Emmett's voice was softer when he spoke again. "There isn't a day that goes by that I don't think about you, Laura. I think about you every day. You make me happy."

Laura smiled even while her father's sobs could still be heard on the phone. That's when she realized once again that God's grace goes far beyond forgiveness. She rejoiced that God brought her to this place of healing. In that old farmhouse on the Texas prairie, where the abuse occurred years before, she gained the victory. What was even more miraculous, God replaced the pain with love. She was free. She gave some of that freedom to her father. She rejoiced in this gift from God. What wonderful power and grace!

Laura's father lived for one more year. During that time, he and Laura continued to talk frequently on the phone, and the fondness between them grew with each call. He passed away in January 1989. Laura was so thankful that the tiny seed of love had grown into a flourishing plant by then, and both of them were blessed by it. She thanked God for their healed relationship.

Mary Sicking died in 2013. Although she was never able to understand Laura and accept that she had become a Protestant, Laura was still thankful that God had given her the opportunity to understand her mother better. She would always admire her mom for the strength of character that had equipped her to endure the difficulties of her life.

Mary Sicking, like Laura and her siblings, was a victim of abuse. For her entire life, Laura blamed her mother for not protecting her. It had taken her many years, but Laura came to realize that her mother did the best she could and that her very presence in their home had softened the difficult situation for her children.

Her mother's strength of character, fortitude, and good money-management skills were a legacy that she passed on to her youngest daughter, and Laura was grateful for that heritage. But most of all, she was grateful for the grace of God that enabled her to forgive both her parents and love them.

CHAPTER 27

....

A Personal Message From Laura

T hank you for reading my story. Each of us has a unique story to tell, and all of us have had challenges and struggles in our lives. With God's help, we can be overcomers. If you or someone close to you has been a victim of abuse or other trauma, then you may find it helpful to know the ideas, activities, and attitudes that helped me to conquer my childhood trauma.

I've arranged these items into six categories of life by the order of their importance to me. In order to overcome, I had to deal with all six of these categories in my life. I've found that when many Christians struggle to triumph over abuse or trauma they deal with only one or two of these areas and often achieve only partial success. In order for me to have the success I wanted in my life, it was absolutely necessary that I deal with all six categories.

Spiritual

This category is the most important to me. Only the power of God in my life enabled me to face my past and deal with my abuse.

Connecting with God through prayer. While the Catholic religion played a somewhat negative role in my early life, the positive presence of God was always there, even when I didn't know it. As a small child, I discovered prayer and cultivated the habit of daily prayer. As my journey toward healing slowly progressed, I found great power in claiming the promises that God has made in the Bible.

Because I recognize that I am weak and lack the knowledge, skills, resources, and wisdom I need to solve many of my problems, I turn to God and beg for

His wisdom, guidance, and help in knowing what to do to navigate the dangerous maze of life. The victories I have achieved have only been accomplished because of my many hours in prayer. Through this power, I have been able to overcome many bad habits that were sabotaging my life. This habit of daily prayer keeps me safe and eliminates my fear of slipping back into my old life. I love this benefit of following Christ.

This life-changing power is available to everyone. You just need to persistently ask for it with all your heart.

Connecting with God through the Bible. Whenever I'm discouraged or depressed, I find much comfort and solace in reading the Bible. In particular, I find peaceful solitude in meditating on the life of Christ and His words. When I read the Bible's stories, I'm encouraged by the great things that God did in other people's lives. I claim the promise that He can do that in my life too.

Avoiding the occult. Through several negative experiences in my past, I learned to avoid anything to do with the occult. It will mislead you and take you down paths where you wouldn't wish to go. I consider it dangerous in many ways.

Mental

This is the one category that links all of the other areas together in a focused approach toward overcoming abuse and trauma.

Recognizing the importance of being focused on the process—not the goal. Because of the dreams God has given me, I believe that I will meet difficult times someday, and I must prepare to stand when all around me falls. This belief has caused me to concentrate on the goal of becoming strong in all six categories of my life but especially on overcoming the effects of abuse that acted as my greatest weakness in times of crisis in the past. This directed approach to life lays over everything I do and especially how I use my free time and my mind. This attitude has given me the will and determination to prevail over my abusive past.

I found that focusing on the process of overcoming and doing what I needed to do day by day ensures that good results and the ultimate goal will take care of themselves. Centering on goals reduced my happiness in the present. At first, when I was working toward a goal, I would say to myself, "I'm not good enough now, but I will be when I reach my goal." Or, "Once I achieve my goal, then I'll be a success and then I'll be happy."

These types of thoughts drained my energy and discouraged me. But when I learned to focus on the process, I would think about the *one* thing I *could* do *at the moment*, instead of the long-term goal of becoming an emotionally healthy person, which would overwhelm me and paralyze me from taking action. So, for example, if my goal was to run a marathon, the process was my running schedule. I didn't have to zero in on the goal of running the whole 26.2 miles; I just focused on running the miles I needed to run that day. This allowed me to enjoy the journey, knowing that the process would lead to the goal.

Choosing leisure-time activities. I believe that how I used my leisure time played a significant role in my ability to triumph over the effects of abuse and trauma, and I continue to be aware of the importance of my choices every day.

I am very careful about what I allow into my mind, whether it is bad self-messaging or what I listen to, watch, or read. I don't waste time by watching merely entertaining television shows or movies. I watch television programs that will inform me in some helpful way.

I'm an avid reader, but I don't read fiction. I love reading the Bible and studying it. In addition, I choose books that give me information that I can use to overcome the challenges of life. Such reading gives me hope and encouragement, along with great information.

I have found certain hobbies and activities to be healing to my spirit, body, and mind. I have always enjoyed running. It has given me both a runner's high and calmed my emotions. Playing the piano privately gives me peaceful rest, especially when I sing my favorite hymns.

All my leisure-time activities and hobbies are chosen to build up and assist my spiritual, mental, physical, medical, emotional, social, and financial development. Finding activities that you enjoy that benefit your spirit, body, and mind can aid the healing process.

Recognizing the importance of patience. It took me many years of work to become emotionally mature enough to go back into my family of origin and deal with the unresolved issues. No matter how much support you have, these things just take time. It is important to be patient with yourself.

Nurturing yourself. As I made progress toward emotional healing and slowly learned to love myself, I realized the importance of nurturing myself and being kind and gentle with myself.

Emotional

With God to lean on, I was able to move through these emotional steps. This is where the hard work takes place.

Recognizing the problem and desiring to overcome it. The first step in surmounting my trauma and abuse was to recognize that my father's behavior was wrong. It was in my first few therapy sessions that I realized that my father's abusive behavior was abnormal, inappropriate, and damaging. At that time, I decided to work for the rest of my life to overcome the damage and to avoid repeating this behavior in my own life. I learned that those who don't reject the abusive behavior of their parent or other perpetrator will identify with him or her and will live to repeat this behavior.

Recognizing the role of therapy. Therapy has been an important part of the healing process for me. I have been fortunate to have had access to several types of therapy. Here is how each one has helped me:

In *psychoanalysis*, I found a setting where I was able to remember past events that my conscious mind had suppressed.

During *behavioral therapy*, I worked with a behavioral therapist to develop a list of things to do when I got a craving for alcohol. These included various activities that redirected my attention away from the craving. For instance, eating lots of salty potato chips was very effective. This made sense years later when I learned that my blood was low in salt.

Cognitive therapy taught me that there are certain attitudes and thought processes that are typical of people who have suffered abuse. Perpetrators can recognize these attitudes. It was important for me to eliminate them, not only for my own mental and emotional health, but also so that perpetrators were unable to target me.

Family system therapy was very helpful. I learned that there were family dynamics that governed the roles and interactions within my family. For instance, if one person starts to get healthy, the family system is threatened. This helped me to understand how the abuse could continue.

In *group therapy*, I learned to talk openly to others about what happened to me and get their feedback. I learned the importance of stopping certain behaviors that were indicators that I had suffered abuse. They included being controlling, having few or no boundaries, having frozen emotions that prevented me from reacting to others in normal ways, addictions, self-hatred, and a lack of trust in other people that caused me to sabotage my relationships.

Embracing my past and accepting my inner child. For most of my life, I have hated myself. I could not forgive myself for what I had experienced as a child. Therapists have repeatedly told me that this is one of the most common outcomes for victims of abuse. For me, this self-hatred took many forms, but the most destructive was constant negative self-messaging. Even when I learned to accept God's forgiveness and love, the negative self-messaging continued, and I still could not love myself. Throughout my life, these negative messages have made me physically ill, causing stabbing pains, nausea, and other symptoms. Of course, this inability to get rid of my self-loathing blocked my emotional and physical healing, and hindered my relationships with others.

I found relief from this problem by the daily practice of looking myself in the mirror and repeating positive affirmations to myself that took the form of: "Even though I was (I list the negative events in my life), I forgive myself, I accept myself, I love myself, and I respect myself, even if no one else does. It doesn't matter. God loves, forgives, and accepts me, and He is the One that I care about. Now, I nurture myself and take care of myself, and love my husband who loves me. Lord, please heal my heart and help me do all these things. Amen."

Over time, I have found this practice to be very effective in eliminating my self-hatred. I no longer suffer from negative self-messaging or self-hatred. The pain and sickness I once experienced whenever I talked or thought of my painful life experiences has gone away completely.

For me, full emotional healing happened when I finally embraced all of my life experiences and acknowledged them as a part of who I am. It happened when I accepted the inner child who experienced those painful events and learned to cherish her.

This was a true victory. It has enabled me to have compassion for others who have also experienced painful periods and to reach out to help them overcome also. By taking this final step toward healing and wholeness, I'm now able to talk openly to others about my experiences and the great things God has done for me.

Physical and medical

My childhood trauma affected more than my emotional health. It also took a terrible toll on my physical well-being. My poor health limited my ability to deal with my emotions, and I had to deal with it in order to make progress.

Taking care of your physical health. I cannot stress enough how important carefully following the eight natural remedies has been to my healing. These principles for living recognize the importance of caring for all aspects of your physical, spiritual, and emotional health. I have spent a great deal of time reading and studying books by Ellen White and other authors who have detailed these eight laws of health (natural remedies) that are usually abbreviated to the following list: proper diet, exercise, pure water, sunlight, temperance, pure air, rest, and trust in God.

While many well-meaning people focus primarily on one or two of these natural remedies—particularly a vegetarian or vegan diet and exercise—my studies and personal experience have convinced me to go much deeper. For instance, I am especially careful about avoiding contaminated water and food. Harmful parasites, bacteria, and viruses can enter your body through such contamination and even through unprotected sex.

I discovered that parasites, for example, can be picked up through eating undercooked meat or through contaminated water. Even if you are a vegetarian, you may unknowingly be ingesting parasites when you eat in restaurants where meat is prepared. Such places may not be careful about preventing meat from coming into contact with other foods, or they may even season their vegetarian dishes with meat juices. I love Asian cuisine, particularly stir-fried vegetarian dishes, but because of the possibility of contamination from undercooked meat or contaminated water, I prefer to prepare it at home.

I avoid eating refined sugar—in particular, sucrose, which I believe drains my body of minerals and causes depression. I also make sure that I get enough protein. (The US government's recommended daily allowance of protein is actually calculated by body weight. For each kilogram of body weight, a person needs 0.8 grams of protein.) Getting sufficient protein keeps my blood sugar balanced, which helps to control moodiness and irritability. I've found that eating lots of high-protein beans, such as pintos, garbanzos, red beans, black beans, kidney beans, and soybeans, makes me feel happy and healthy, so I eat them often!

Recognizing environmental factors and their impact on emotional health. Learning about certain medically related factors that can affect my emotions helped me to minimize the emotional impact of past abuse. In my case, I learned that my body contained high levels of mercury and that this chemical can cause depression.

I wondered, *How did mercury find its way into my body?* Through my reading and from information supplied by my doctors, I learned to avoid eating fish; getting or having silver dental amalgam fillings; wearing sunscreen; using antibacterial soap; and using certain face, hand, and body creams (I learned to look for ingredients with the prefixes *cinni* and *merc*). I am also very careful about taking prescription drugs because some may contain mercury or other metals.

Many of the multi-minerals in drugstores or health food stores contain contaminants of mercury, lead, and other heavy metals, which make them worse than taking no multi-minerals at all. Because of this contamination issue, it is important to have a trained doctor specify which multi-mineral supplement is contamination free. Based on my doctors' recommendation, I have been taking Simply Natural's Simply minerals for the past twenty years. Prior to that, I've had other doctors recommend TheraTech or MezoTrace multi-minerals. These are contamination free also.

If you test positive for high mercury levels, the mercury can be removed from your body through chelation therapy. For me, chelation improved how I felt and made my emotions more positive. I've had many such treatments through the years and will no doubt continue them for the rest of my life. You can check out the Web site of the American College for Advancement in Medicine to find a chelation clinic near you.

I discovered that low mineral levels can sometimes cause depression. Taking a strong multimineral supplement can eliminate this some of the time. Having good levels of healthy minerals in my body has dramatically helped me to avoid absorbing mercury and has promoted a happier attitude.

I also became aware that I needed to rid my body of parasites. Most of us carry parasites in our bodies, and certain parasites can have a negative impact on physical health as well as affect our emotions. It is best to eliminate them from the body.

Social

Emotional trauma and damage, unless dealt with, can take a terrible toll on one's ability to sustain healthy relationships. I found that working on this category helped me to make progress in all of the others.

Connecting with God and with people through the Sabbath. I use the Sabbath day as a special time to heal and grow relationships, both with God and my fellow humans. Having a specific day set aside for this purpose has helped me to develop the habit of calling family members every Saturday morning just to see how they are doing.

Going to church and socializing with other church members is my regular Sabbath routine. I find that this gives me good practice in relationship building, and it creates opportunities to learn conflict resolution in a less-demanding environment than at work or with family.

Recognizing the gift of human relationships. I was told in therapy that the age you were when the abuse began is the age at which your emotional development was frozen. For me, I believe this was when I was about two years old. I have been so fortunate to have a strong, supportive husband who has played an important role in my ability to mature emotionally. In his kind and loving way, he tells me things that no one else can get away with, which helps me to grow and mature.

I've also had friends through the years who have identified with my experiences and encouraged me to emotional maturity. I count my husband and my friends as gifts from God, granted to me when I had little to offer them but needed them most.

Financial

Recognizing education and occupation. While this category might not seem obvious at first, I found it to be important. At the age of fourteen, I determined to get a good education in order to become a strong, independent woman. Earning a chemical-engineering degree and having a well-paid position has provided me with a good income, which has enabled me to pay for therapy and have financial security. In addition, it has given me a sense of identity and self-respect. I would recommend a similar path for any young person, regardless of his or her background.

EPILOGUE

....

Laura developed a rewarding career as an environmental engineer with the US Army Corps of Engineers. She is responsible for determining the amount of water that spills over the hydroelectric dams on the Columbia and Snake Rivers in the Pacific Northwest, which ensures that endangered salmon successfully migrate to the ocean. The spill program that Laura works in has been involved in litigation regarding the Endangered Species Act for many years. Laura performs computer modeling as part of the technical support for responses to the court as well as for daily spill decisions. She is involved in writing court reports that are required as part of the litigation.

Greg has a successful career as the Public Affairs and Religious Liberty director at the North Pacific Union Conference of Seventh-day Adventists. He builds and works with coalitions to write and pass religious freedom bills in the state legislatures of Alaska, Idaho, Montana, Oregon, and Washington.

Greg and Laura are thankful that the Lord continues to guide and direct in their marriage, and they have celebrated thirty-two years of happiness together. Both are active in their local church, and they continue to fund the education of many young people. Laura continues to pray earnestly that God will always lead in her life and eagerly looks forward to whatever work God has in mind for her in the future.